The HR Change Toolkit

Your Complete Guide to Making it Happen

Lucy A

First published in Great Britain by Practical Inspiration Publishing, 2019

© Lucy Adams, 2019

The moral rights of the author have been asserted

ISBN 978-1-78860-043-9

Every effort has been made to trace copyright holders and to obtain their permission for the use of copyright material. The publisher apologizes for any errors or omissions and would be grateful if notified of any corrections that should be incorporated in future reprints or editions of this book.

 Practical Inspiration
PUBLISHING

Contents

The Frustration of Change

If you've ever tried to make waves as an HR professional I'm guessing this is roughly how it went. You came up with an idea — let's say it was to encourage employees to move between business divisions more regularly, creating a fluid and dynamic culture. To make this happen, you explained to your senior leaders what you wanted and why it would be a good thing. They loved the notion and instructed their managers to action it without delay. This worked a treat, and within six months the proportion of posts filled internally by candidates from a different division increased by 30 percent. Everyone was delighted.

This never happens.

Instead, it probably went more like this. You came up with the idea, or were tasked with it by your Chief Executive, and approached the leadership team. They nodded, said it sounded great, and then went away and... did nothing. Or you created a process called 'Let's Move Around', with managers completing forms to explain why they had or hadn't taken someone on from a different division. The result was a disappointing 20 percent compliance rate on the form filling, accompanied by a stubborn and mysterious aversion to recruiting from outside their areas. Everyone was frustrated.

It's hard to make change happen in HR, isn't it? After all, there's no point having bright ideas if you can't implement them. Despite this, there seems to be plenty of guidance out there about *what* we HR professionals should be doing differently, but when it comes to *how* we should do it, the gurus are less helpful. This book fills that gap, by helping you understand why people don't like to change the way they work and how you can make it easier for both them and you.

But first I have a confession to make: I'm a recovering HR Director. I've spent 20 years in the field and have been HR Director at three sizeable organisations: large-scale service provider Serco, global law firm Eversheds, and finally the BBC. For the past four years, however, I've been engaged in something rather different. Having become increasingly frustrated with my profession towards the end of my time at the BBC I realised it was time for a change of my own, which led to the creation of my consultancy, Disruptive HR. Together with my business partner, Karen Moran, I now work with HR professionals all over the world who both recognise the need to change the way HR operates and want help with doing it. I've met thousands of HR folk through my workshops and consultancy programmes, and while they're a diverse bunch they all have one thing in common: an overwhelming desire to do HR differently. They understand that the macro business environment is experiencing tumultuous change and that they therefore need to wise up to a different way of working; in some cases their leaders are pushing for this too. But to their frustration, their attempts at making this transition a reality are largely unsuccessful.

I've certainly had my fair share of failures when I've tried to improve the way HR goes about things. When I was at Serco each division was focused on its own sector: defence, rail, prisons, and so on. I could see there was growth potential in helping teams work together rather than separately in siloes, and I wanted to encourage this. My first move was to remove the financial incentive for managers to focus only on their own areas, by instigating a new bonus scheme which combined a reward for individual achievement with the needs of the wider company. This would be the ideal solution (or so I thought). Unfortunately, the result was a hugely complicated bonus structure in which leaders were financially incentivised according to group, divisional, and personal performance. Not only was it ungainly but it also had no business impact whatsoever because no-one could understand it, and by the time the bonus amounts were split into the different areas they became irrelevant. All I achieved was a waste of time and effort, and the resentment of leaders and managers who couldn't understand why I was tinkering with something they thought worked perfectly well already. Zero points to me for that one.

I had another disappointing experience with implementing change when I tried to simplify the pay and grading structure at the BBC. My aim was to reduce and harmonise the 5,000 job titles across the organisation to make it easier for people to contemplate shifting from one division to another. This would result in a more dynamic BBC, with a flatter hierarchy. Together with my team I devised what I thought was a beautiful and transformative plan. We slaved for nine months crafting a revised grading structure that was reduced from 17 levels to 6, cutting the number of job titles (eliminating 'senior' and 'executive', for instance), and slotting them into neat, new pay bands. We could have saved ourselves the trouble — it bombed. Why? Because I'd completely overlooked two vital elements that were important to people. The first was that employees liked their tribal language, and didn't want to relinquish it for what they saw as HR expediency. The second was that in an era of cost cutting and low pay increases, the puffing-up of a job title with the addition of 'senior' served as a reward in its own right. I'd also missed the whole point of the exercise: the reason people didn't readily move across divisions was little to do with a lack of understanding about job roles, and more to do with the fact that it wasn't culturally acceptable to 'jump ship' from, say, television to radio. It was seen as disloyal. And our response to that? To snatch away people's hard-won job status, and in the process alienate them from HR even further. This was brought home to me when I presented my simplified structure to a wall of ill-disguised apathy at the World Service senior team: 'I'm not sure this does anything except achieve HR neatness,' I was told. They were right.

I recount these sorry tales to show how, when we in HR fail to understand the human reasons why people are wedded to the way things are now, we also fail to create the change we want. My motivation was sound in each case but the method was wrong; all I did was swop one process that at least worked to a degree, for another that didn't work at all. It was certainly rational and made sense intellectually, but it ignored the human factor, and given that we're supposed to be the 'human experts' in HR this was somewhat ironic. Yet again I'd put my faith in the established wisdom that inventing and changing processes can transform human behaviour, and yet again I'd neglected to understand the importance of how human beings think, feel and behave.

You'll be gathering by now that to make change more successful in HR, we need to radically redesign the way we do it. In my last book, *HR: Disrupted,*[1] I explored the reasons for this and towards the end gave some guidance on how to achieve it. However, while I'm delighted with how much the book has helped people, I've always considered the 'how to' section at the end to be its weakest because at that point I hadn't fully engaged with the practicalities of

---

[1] *HR Disrupted: It's Time for Something Different,* by Lucy Adams. Practical Inspiration Publishing, 2017.

HR change. Now I've had more time to develop my thinking in this area I've written this one, which is about *how* to make change happen. Be warned, though — the solid tips and advice you'll find here will lead you to undertake a radical remodelling of your own back yard, because we in HR can only make a lasting difference if we're willing to take a fresh look at how we work too. In fact the test of this book will be if it helps you change your own HR department, as well as your organisation, for the better.

The insights about change I'm going to share with you are not all original. You won't find a raft of novel change management theories, or wacky ways to make things better. But what you will find is a host of adaptations found in other disciplines such as Marketing, Product Design, and Psychology, from which HR can borrow and steal for our own purposes. What's more, I'll take the concepts of how 'stuff happens' in these areas of expertise and put them into an HR context for you.

Let's consider Marketing first. Marketing know-how is useful for HR, because people in that discipline understand, often far better than we do, how to influence human attitudes and behaviour. However, we've not traditionally seen this area as our natural ally in business. Instead that's been Finance, from which we've traditionally taken our lead in terms of insight and data analysis, operational compliance, and efficiency. This has led us to view people as assets rather than as living, breathing individuals. Many of my tips in this book are based on how to put this right, because I see understanding how to influence human behaviour as a high priority.

Product Design is another area we can learn from. In HR we tend to see ourselves as providing a service, priding ourselves on creating consistent, cost-effective, scalable, and easy-to-monitor processes that can be applied across the whole organisation. This sounds good, but it isn't. To put it another way, we create and tinker with processes that support our service rather than asking ourselves if the process is actually needed in the first place. In contrast, product designers base everything on their end users and this has produced an increasingly agile discipline which isn't hindered by the same rigid procedures as we have in HR. If you think about it, can you honestly say there's much at all about HR that has changed in recent years?

We also have a huge amount to learn from psychologists and behavioural economists. It amazes me how shy we are about calling ourselves the human experts, and again this comes down to our age-old desire to emulate Finance. In a world in which CEOs and shareholders are looking for certainty, we've tried to boost our status by proving our financial benefit to our organisations. This means instead of becoming experts in the messy, intangible world of human behaviour, we've become specialists in process design and project implementation. I can certainly understand why, because it comes from a desire to help people work more effectively, but it's not the way to create effective change.

As a profession we're still inexperienced in using new technology to help us do a better job; a recent Deloitte survey revealed only 16 percent of companies are ready to manage a workforce in which new technologies and people work side by side.[2] When I think about how few HR people I come across who are savvy with social media or any other form of digital technology, this worries me; we don't need to be experts but we do at least need to see its potential for recruitment and learning.

---

[2] https://www2.deloitte.com/uk/en/pages/press-releases/
articles/companies-unprepared-for-digital-disruption.html

This book isn't about change theory — there are plenty of those already. Rather, it's an up-to-date guide to the cutting-edge learnings about change that are coming out right now, and a step-by-step guide to applying them in HR. You'll gain a practical toolkit along the way, central to which is my accompanying downloadable workbook which you can access at https://disruptivehr.com/thehrchangetoolkitworkbook. This will give you a place to note down your ideas and also to work through some simple exercises so it becomes a template for your own plans for change. Once you've finished reading you'll have a strategy in place ready to go.

We'll start by taking a brief tour through the current business landscape and look at why HR needs to change its approach if it's to be successful in transforming its organisations. Then we'll cover what you can do to get your own HR team ready, as well as how to prepare the ground in your organisation. After that you'll learn ways to design your change and how to help it to work far more quickly, easily, and — most importantly — effectively than what you've tried so far. You'll also read a sample case study about an HR leader who's made change work for her in a particular area, so you can see how it can succeed in practice.

If there's one thing I've learned in my journey through disrupting HR in various organisations, it's that it doesn't have to be as big and scary as you think. In fact it's better if it's not, because when you as an HR professional feel confident about change, everyone else will too. It really is down to you to lead the way, and here's how to do it.

Section 1

EACH of Us Has a Role to Play

Imagine you're in a boat in a storm. The wind is howling, the waves are crashing, and you're not sure if you're going to make it to shore. But help is at hand — along comes a lifeboat and the captain throws you a ring. The problem is, you need to dive into the water to reach it. You know you can't stay where you are because that's only going to end one way and that float is the key to your survival, but on the other hand it feels risky to jump in and at least give yourself a chance.

Many of the HR professionals I talk to say this is a bit how it feels to be working in HR right now. There's unfamiliar technology to grapple with, evolving expectations at all levels to cater for, and the never-ending demands of CEOs and Finance Directors to live up to. It's not that you don't appreciate the need for change and may even feel excited about it, but it can feel overwhelming at times. You know it's time to let go of traditional ways of working but moving to something different feels a bit like taking an unwelcome dip in the icy sea. Surely it's better to sit tight and wait it out for now.

What could make this easier? For a start, it's helpful to gain an overview of the transformations taking place in the world of work. The notion of organisational change is nothing new but if you'll let me take you on a whistle-stop tour of what's happening and why, you'll see why HR needs to position itself as a leader in these uncharted waters. This section aims to set the scene so you can do just that.

The changes we face

Technological challenges

We can start with developments in technology, which are altering business more rapidly and profoundly than most of us can keep up with — and that goes for pretty much anyone, not just us in HR. Never more than now have organisations needed agile and innovative leaders to steer them through these unsettling changes. Unfortunately, if we were to ask ourselves if we're helping them develop these capabilities, we'd have to draw the conclusion we could do better. Instead, we tend to be more concerned with driving down costs and maintaining the status quo than with encouraging our employees to make the most of what technology can offer.

Novel ways of serving customers

Familiar companies are increasingly not what they seem: supermarkets are turning into banks and online retailers into media companies, to mention just a couple of examples. Businesses are increasingly realising their goal is to serve their end customers in whatever way they want, which means that collaboration between organisations, and internally between departments, is becoming increasingly common. This is leading to some interesting conversations at boardroom and department manager level. Is your team helping your leaders to manage this shift? If you're like the majority of HR Managers I speak with, I suspect not.

Evolving working practices

First came the influx of millennials, with different expectations of the world of work to their forebears. Next, the gig economy and the use of artificial intelligence burst onto the scene. All these trends are changing the nature of jobs. Without flexibility in working practices, we find it hard to satisfy the expectations of multi-generational teams, to say nothing of those working across varying time zones and cultures. People are also evolving their expectations of the length of time they want to work for,

and how. Motivating and managing these fluidities involves treating employees less homogeneously than we've
traditionally done, and more as individuals. Yet I don't
see this happening on a meaningful scale.

New-style leadership

And finally, what does leadership mean to us today?
The transparency created by social media, coupled with
the general lowering of automatic respect for those in
authority, has led to an atmosphere of distrust towards
those in charge. In many cases this is justified. The damaging of employment brands by unethical CEO and executive behaviour isn't easy to recover from, and prospec-
tive employees are less and less likely to want to work for
organisations that don't behave according to their own
values. Even when our leaders do behave ethically, we in
HR need to recognise that employees trust people 'like
them' rather than those who take a command-and-control approach.

I'm sure none of this is new to you, and it's likely you'll
have a raft of your own more specific organisational challenges that you could tell me about. But what has your
HR department done to adapt and — just as importantly
— to anticipate them? I'm not referring to sticking-plas-
ter remedies such as appointing a 'Head of Transformation' or re-jigging the gradings for your annual appraisal
system. I'm talking about fundamentally rethinking how
you're equipping your organisation for the future.

It comes to this: we can't keep saying the world of
work has changed but keep doing (and thinking about)
HR in the same old way. If we don't move more quickly
than other people in our organisations by jumping into
those waves and grabbing the life-ring, we'll be forever
branded as the department that's floundering and failing
to catch up. It may feel overwhelming at first, but the rest

of this book will give you the tools and techniques to help you challenge both your own assumptions and those of your company. Stick with me and put on your life jacket, because it's going to be a fascinating adventure.

But first, you'll need some principles to work with.

The EACH model

If you've read my previous book, *HR Disrupted*, the EACH model will be familiar to you. Feel free to skip the rest of this chapter if that's you, although refreshing your memory is not a bad idea. If you're not familiar with it please read on, as this model summarises my principles of what HR should be like if it's to remain relevant and even become respected. I appreciate it may make you feel uncomfortable and you might think certain aspects of it have nothing to do with you. But I'm equally confident you'll be nodding your head at various points, and if the odd rueful laugh escapes your lips while you're doing so that's great.

HR needs to undergo fundamental change if it's to enable organisations to lead, manage, and train the people they need for the future, so let's look at what that transformation could look like. There are three elements to this: we in HR must start treating our **E**mployees as **A**dults, **C**onsumers, and **H**uman beings. This is a radical new way of seeing our role, and it applies not only to what we need to do to make change happen, but also how we do it. I'll take each of the three elements of Adult, Consumer, and Human in turn.

Employees as Adults

When we think of the relationship HR has with the employees in our organisations, what's the first word that springs to mind? Is it 'trust'? Probably not. In fact, in most companies the default setting is more likely to be one of parent to child.

This takes two forms. The first is that of HR seeing staff as children who must be protected from themselves, such as when we manage every aspect of their careers or put up posters in the bathrooms saying 'Now Wash Your Hands'. I dub this approach 'Employer Mum' (forgive the gender stereotyping) because she likes to take an overly protective role. The second is that of HR seeing all employees as potential troublemakers who could harm our organisations, such as when we write multi-page policy documents that nobody reads or bestow grades on people at their end-of-term school report (the annual appraisal). I call this approach 'Employer Dad' because he's the critical parent.

What's wrong with this? For a start, when we don't have confidence in employees either being able to think for themselves or behaving well, we irritate and patronise the vast majority who are capable of both. It also has more serious consequences because a non-trusting environment makes it hard for people to take risks, challenge authority, and try something new; and that, as we've seen from the changes sweeping through our workplaces, is a killer for innovation, progress, and even survival.

We could start from a place of trust instead of control. When we do this we find our employees are more likely to behave in a responsible, productive, creative, and forward-thinking way. We could even encourage them to take increasing accountability for progressing their careers, thereby fostering their enthusiasm for improving their performances. And if we were to wrap this up in communications which treat them as intelligent adults, we'd likely be surprised by the resourcefulness and wisdom they show in return.

Employees as Consumers

When creating a strategy, successful consumer companies always start with their market and then work backwards. We never hear their Marketing Directors express the wish that their customers would behave differently; instead, they find out what those customers want and make sure they provide it. If we were to apply a similarly consumer-based thinking to the way we see our employees, we'd experience a radical shift in our assumptions. For a start, we'd realise we need to understand more about them as individuals, rather than seeing them as a homogeneous group. This would lead to us moving away from one-size-fits-all processes designed to suit HR, and towards flexible systems that treat them as clusters of people with differing wants and needs.

The problem is, most organisations don't know much about the people who are supposedly their most important assets: their employees. This is because we in HR don't use the right tools and techniques to find out. Instead of the pointless annual engagement survey (when did that ever produce anything useful?) we could encourage managers to check in with their staff more frequently or carry out some qualitative research across the business.

Segmenting our employee base is critical to developing services that meet everyone's needs. If we don't do this, people will feel disengaged from our processes and act grudgingly instead of with full commitment. Nowhere is this more evident than in the annual appraisal process, a classic uniform procedure. Research shows 92 percent of companies do them, but that only 8 percent believe they're worth the time and effort — that's a huge waste of time and resources. Once we know more about our employee segments we can design processes around our users, instead of around our own convenience and desire to control.

Employees as Human beings

My encouragement to treat employees as adults and consumers could be directed as much at the leaders around our organisations as it could at ourselves. But not treating employees as human beings is an area in which HR really has made a rod for its own back. As a profession we need to put the human back into human resources, by developing a deeper understanding of how employees think and feel, and also by considering how we can create more human leaders at the same time.

If you want to understand more about the human brain and how it works, there's a wealth of resources available. David Rock's SCARF model,[3] for instance, shows how people respond negatively to threats to their status, sense of certainty, autonomy, ability to relate to others, and perceptions of fairness. When these elements are rewarded instead of threatened, people are freed up to work more effectively. Take a moment to consider whether the majority of our HR activities are designed to create either threats or rewards. Do they centre on generating policies and procedures which reduce autonomy? Do they create a parent-child dynamic which reduces a sense of status? And do they impose structural changes, which upset people's feelings of certainty and fairness? My guess is that threats, rather than rewards, are the rule.

So what does motivate people? Dan Pink's research-based book *Drive*[4] explains how we're all intrinsically motivated, and questions whether extrinsic rewards,

---

[3] *Your Brain at Work*, by David Rock. HarperCollins, 2009. Also http://web.archive.org/web/20100705024057/http://www. your-brain-at-work.com/files/NLJ_SCARFUS.pdf

[4] *Drive: The Surprising Truth About What Motivates Us*, by Daniel H. Pink. Riverhead Books, 2011.

such as money, are as worthwhile as we assume. He says there are three internal drivers which make us want to work productively: autonomy (the ability to control our lives and work), mastery (the chance to become better at what we're good at), and meaning (having a sense of higher purpose about what we do). How much time do we spend developing our employees' sense of autonomy, mastery, and meaning? In my experience as an HR Director, I'd say it's not a lot.

How does HR measure up?

You may be feeling a level of resistance to these arguments, and I get that, because it's only after a few years of developing this thinking that I've been able to embrace its relevance. The EACH model is designed to help companies survive in a disrupted world, so it's inevitable some of it will feel uncomfortable. A good place to start is to evaluate how it relates to your organisation, by taking my 10-minute diagnostic test at https://disruptivehr. com/each-hr-diagnostic. Over the past two years almost 1,000 HR professionals from a wide variety of countries and sectors have completed it. The results show two thirds of respondents have a predominantly parental approach to their employees, and the area in which they're least effective is in treating their staff as consumers (72 percent use one-size-fits-all processes without any kind of meaningful customisation). So you're not alone in struggling with these issues, and it will be interesting to see how you compare.

Here's the link to the diagnostic again: https://disruptivehr.com/each-hr-diagnostic.

It's not just what we do, it's the way that we do it

There's good news ahead: we can now move onto what you can do about this situation, and I promise you it's plenty. But first, let me make one important point: I'm sure there's much you want to change in your organisation, but it's *how* you go about doing it that's just as important. This means you need to take off your HR hat for a while and don one from marketing or product development instead. So abandon the idea of rolling out a top-down change programme, for instance, which would be the old-style, parental way of implementing transformation. Instead, open yourself up to finding new ways of achieving what you want by customising your actions to different audiences, and by factoring in how humans think, feel, and behave. These alternative methods are actually a lot more fun and exciting to implement than the old ones, and — crucially — they work.

Action points

- Take the diagnostic test for your own organisation at https://disruptivehr.com/each-hr-diagnostic and discover your own company's EACH profile.

- Record this in your workbook, which you can download at https://disruptivehr.com/thehrchangetoolkitworkbook.

- Consider visiting our blog, which contains lots of implementation tips for the EACH model in all areas of HR: https://disruptivehr.com/blogs-podcasts-webinars.

Quick recap

- Workplaces are changing at a fundamental level and have been for some time, but we in HR aren't equipping leaders and managers to thrive in this new world.

- When we treat employees as children we reduce their willingness to take risks and innovate; treating them as adults gives them the confidence to cope with change more easily.

- When we treat employees as recipients of one-size-fits-all processes and procedures we stifle their ability to work effectively; providing them with products and services designed around their particular needs frees them from pointless and harmful restrictions.

- When we treat employees as assets or machines we demotivate them and make it hard for them to do their best work; treating them as human beings encourages their innate ability to adapt to change in a positive way.

- As you think about what you're going to change, consider first *how* you're going to do it and with what mindset. Your thinking must alter before your behaviour can.

Section 2

Why HR Finds Change Hard

If you've ever tried to get one person to change the way they do something, you know how difficult it can be. I must have asked my husband not to leave his stuff on the stairs a hundred times, but still he does it. Likewise, no matter how often my PA has suggested I give her more than a week's notice for planning my business trips, I can never seem to factor this into my thinking. If it's this tricky when you want to affect one person, how much more challenging is it when you're trying to transform an entire organisation involving hundreds or thousands of people? Of course, it's going to be hard.

Organisations haven't made it any easier for themselves over the years. If you've been on a change management course or read much about how to effect organisational change, you've probably been fed a highly rational approach to the process. For instance, back in 2003 consultants at McKinsey[5] suggested four conditions had to be present before employees would change their behaviour:

- a compelling story so people could grasp the point of the change;
- the CEO and senior leadership modelling the change themselves;
- all systems and processes to be aligned to encourage the desired new behaviour; and
- the training and skills being in place to help people to work differently.

It sounds terribly sensible, doesn't it? This type of thinking has been accepted for years and in many cases still is, because it appeals to our sense of reason. Unfortunately, it doesn't work. In his seminal 1996 book *Leading*

---

[5] *The Psychology of Change Management*, by Emily Lawson and Colin Price, 2003. https://www.mckinsey.com/business-functions/organization/our-insights/the-psychology-of-change-management

Change, John Kotter revealed that only 30 percent of change management programmes achieve what they set out to do, and a newer 2008 McKinsey survey of 3,199 executives around the world confirmed this when it found that only one in three succeeds.[6] This is because rather than being logical, change is an emotional and irrational process, and there's an emerging school of thought that recognises this. In a later McKinsey article, 'The Irrational Side of Change Management',[7] Carolyn Aitken and Scott Keller present a more helpful view of what human beings respond to when it comes to change. It turns out there are several elements to this, and below I go through a selection of them, along with some of my own findings from years of trying to get businesses to change the way they work.

Here's what makes it hard for HR to effect change.

The stories that work for bosses don't necessarily work for employees

Remember the McKinsey's 'compelling stories' I mentioned earlier, that are considered so essential to persuade the rank and file to change? They don't work across the board because — surprise, surprise — not everyone responds to the same information in the same way. Senior leaders tend to tell the story of the financial or competitive reasons for change, but research by a number of leading thinkers in the social sciences has shown that when managers and employees are asked what motivates them most in their work, they're equally split between

---

6 https://www.mckinsey.com/business-functions/organization/our-insights/the-irrational-side-of-change-management

7 'The Irrational Side of Change Management', by Carolyn Aitken and Scott Keller, 2009. https://www.mckinsey.com/business-functions/organization/our-insights/the-irrational-side-of-change-management

five forms of impact: that on society, the customer, the company, the team, and 'me'. It seems it's not as simple as providing an irresistible business rationale for change, because this only hits one out of the five impacts that matter to people. In other words, it's not a one-size-fits-all process, although that's the way it's usually treated.

Individual leaders are less influential than key groups of employees

In any change initiative I've ever been involved with the assumption was always that the leaders needed to stand up and lead the change. But when you consider how much less trusted leaders are even than they were a few years ago (the Edelman Trust Barometer[8] showed a drop of 12 points globally for CEOs in 2017), it stands to reason that employees would be readier to put their faith in people 'like them' — they're easier to relate to, for a start. This tallies with the growing trend of believing in our peers more than in professional and technical experts. I don't know about you, but I trust a restaurant review on TripAdvisor from someone I've never met more than I do the restaurant's own PR. Personally I find our lack of faith in experts worrying and sometimes a little frustrating, but it's a factor we have to take into consideration.

Reinforcing mechanisms such as money are less effective than we think

I'll admit, whenever I led a change management programme in the past I almost always included a financial reward element — it seemed the obvious way to incentivise compliance. Along with other leaders I assumed we

---

[8] See the 2017 findings here: https://www.edelman.co.uk/magazine/posts/edelman-trust-barometer-2017-uk-findings/

simply needed to provide a clear, compelling rationale for change, get the leaders to communicate it, and then bonus people according to their participation. However, I now know money isn't usually effective as a reinforcing mechanism, at least on a long-term basis. In my last book, *HR Disrupted*, I explained in detail why traditional financial bonuses don't work. I'm not the only one who thinks this way: Dan Pink's *Drive*[9] and Margaret Heffernan's *Wilful Blindness*[10] also prove this point, and I've taken much of my inspiration from them and their research.

Perceptions of fairness have a higher importance to people than rational choice or self-interest

The rational view is that all you have to do to make change happen is to appeal to employees' self-interest and then pay them to comply. Social scientist Danah Zohar, however, says perceptions of fairness have a far higher importance than rational choice, and that people will even act against their self-interest if the new system they're being asked to adopt crosses their personal values. I even know a few senior leaders who've been offered pay rises, but who felt so strongly they were inequitable that they didn't take them. People won't always go for fairness over self-interest, but they certainly find it demotivating when they see others suffer unduly.

Our leaders are still looking for certainty

Recently I was asked to speak at a high-level leadership conference. 'Great,' I thought, 'I can talk about why HR

---

[9] *Drive: The Surprising Truth About What Motivates Us*, by Daniel H. Pink. Riverhead Books, 2011.

[10] *Wilful Blindness: Why We Ignore the Obvious at Our Peril*, by Margaret Heffernan. Simon & Schuster UK, 2012.

needs to change.' That was until I discovered the topic: *Key HR Trends Over the Next 10 Years.* Needless to say, I declined. Quite how they thought I was supposed to predict anything that far ahead I have no idea, and it reflects the obsession organisations have with being able to foretell the distant future. Chief executives, leadership teams, non-executive directors, and shareholders continue to be intolerant of surprises or ambiguity. Instead they want certainty around numbers, operational plans, and people (or as they like to call them, 'assets'). To guide them in their predictions they look to HR for assurances around skills, capabilities, and employee numbers for resource planning.

Unfortunately, we in HR are guilty of facilitating this fear of the future, as we scramble to provide the figures we're asked for in a bid to prove our worth. Then we realise the only way we can deliver the numbers is by instigating processes. These enable us to tell the CEO the number of courses our employees have been on, for instance, but not whether this training has resulted in a long-term rise in performance. If we were to focus on the latter rather than the former, we wouldn't be able to deliver the black and white figures the CEO was after. Perhaps we should get more comfortable with uncertainty, because if all it achieves is the creation of processes which encourage poor results, what's the value in it? Bold words, but ones that are not easy to voice at the boardroom table.

Leaders often believe they're not the ones who need to change

We like to think of our leaders as being role models, but so often I've sat in meetings in which leaders have agreed, 'Absolutely, this needs to change,' and yet it's clear they assume this doesn't apply to them. A recent research study[11] amongst more than 3,600 leaders across a variety of roles and industries revealed that the more power a leader holds, the more likely they are to overestimate their skills and abilities. This poses a problem when we want to effect change, because the very people most influential in our organisations are the ones least likely to believe they need to alter the way they think.

Alongside this inner blindness is the touching belief held by many Chief Executives and leaders that they're the 'human experts', because they're people themselves. I remember a conversation I had with a lovely, open-minded guy who'd previously been head of logistics and planning at a major telecomms company. He moved into an HR directorship role and was asked his view on the pay increases that should have been implemented earlier that year. Just as he would have done in logistics he put together a board paper with recommendations, presented it to the board, and expected it to be passed without argument. He was the expert, used to being listened to. To his amazement his pay rise analysis sparked a huge debate around the boardroom table, entirely based on other directors' personal views, anecdotes, and assumptions about what was affordable. This illustrates how hard it is to be listened to as an HR authority when everyone else thinks they're people experts too.

Bosses find it difficult to see anything wrong with what we're doing now

If you were around in the 1980s take a moment to remember what it was like then; I cringe when I cast my mind back to the scary haircuts and shoulder pads. That

---

[11] Read the full article here, it's fascinating: https://hbr.org/2018/01/what-self-awareness-really-is-and-how-to-cultivate-it

era feels like ancient history now, and yet it's also when performance management in its current form evolved. So that's almost 40 years of annual gradings and ratings linked to bonuses.[12] Ten years later the first annual engagement surveys, along with research company Gallup, were born. It's no wonder, then, that if you know anyone in a senior leadership role in their 40s or 50s they'll have been steeped in this approach to management since the day they started work. The very fact they're at the top suggests they've benefited from the status quo, with their bonuses based on high ratings and the rigid succession planning process that propelled them up the ladder. Why would they see the need to change any of this?

What's more, too often leaders can't see what's wrong with the established system because they're not the ones feeling the pain it causes. For instance, in his book *What Matters Now*, Gary Hamel[13] makes the interesting point that CEOs and board directors are less likely to experience bureaucratic barriers to change than others in their companies, because they're not the ones having to battle through them. When I wanted to hire someone as HR Director, for example, I would ask one of my team to spend the required hours doing the paperwork, with the result that I never realised how awful it was to get approval for a new hire. If there's no recognition of the need for change, and little appetite to promote it, apathy results.

---

[12] There's a great timeline here: https://hbr.org/2016/10/the-performance-management-revolution

[13] You can read an interesting article by Gary Hamel and Michele Zanini about bureaucratic barriers here: https://hbr.org/2017/08/what-we-learned-about-bureaucracy-from-7000-hbr-readers

Organisations see change as a linear activity and so does HR

When I was HR Director at the BBC I remember the meetings I'd have with leaders to discuss the various changes going on. Their continual plea was, 'When are these things going to settle down?' To them stasis was the default setting, with change being imposed upon it and having a beginning, middle, and end. An announcement would be made, the change explained, and processes and systems put in place to make sure it happened; at some point, the transformation would be 'done'. I can't blame the leaders because HR hasn't done anything to counter this linear approach. We've encouraged it through our reliance on long-term planning horizons, managing transformation in a controlled way so anticipated behavioural change is even built into the calendar. We generate Gantt charts galore and even recruit programme managers to control the process, because we don't trust employees to manage it themselves.

Another way in which we have a flawed approach to change is when we see it in terms of the structural hierarchy, implementing it in a top-down way through divisions, departments, and operational teams. In reality, organisations are more complex than that. Working relationships happen dynamically and organically, which means HR's cascaded change communications and activities are based on an organisational structure that doesn't exist anymore.

HR takes a parental approach to change

When it comes to motivating people to change, HR's underpinning assumption is that, just as we would coerce a child to tidy their room each day by nagging them until it's done, our employees don't like change and therefore won't do it unless we make them. Let's take performance management as an example. The original idea behind it was to enable each employee to have a regular conversation with their manager, so they could perform a bit better tomorrow than today. This was a worthy endeavour, but we never trusted managers to do it so we created a process which forced them to appraise their teams at least once a year. Lo and behold, the performance management process was born. Then we realised we didn't rely on managers to do it well enough, so we created a ratings structure for them to follow. Funnily enough people didn't appreciate being labelled with numbers, so we changed them to phrases like 'meets expectations', complete with detailed explanatory notes for managers to get their heads around. Soon we saw many employees achieving consistently high ratings. Suspecting their managers were avoiding giving lower ones because they didn't want to have difficult conversations, we forced everyone to follow a distribution curve; guided distribution was born. And the result? All hell broke loose because everyone hated it. But we didn't stop there. We realised our managers didn't like using the *system*. 'Ah, it's the platform!' we thought. 'That's easy to fix.' This led us to purchase expensive online performance management technology, which finally baked the process into the HR corporate system so firmly that changing it would be like extracting a fossil from a rock.

We didn't mean for it to end like this. From the starting point all we wanted to achieve was a small behavioural change, and yet we're now further away than ever from managers and their staff having frequent and helpful conversations. The end result is people's performance and motivation don't seem to have improved much over the years, because all we've done is to make a process that was flawed to begin with more efficient and controlled.

What could we have achieved if we'd invested even one percent of the billions we've wasted on these systems, into finding new ways of having useful conversations? These could include feedback through well-facilitated peer-to-peer reviews, helpful prompts for line managers to have frequent check-ins, and employee-led conversations. Unfortunately, our top-down parental approach has blinded us to these options, making change difficult to facilitate.

Resistance to change is normal

As I mentioned when I summarised David Rock's SCARF model in the last chapter, we humans typically don't like change. We react to it as a threat to our status, sense of certainty, ability to work autonomously, stability in terms of who we work with, and feelings about fairness. So let's not kid ourselves that transformation is ever going to be easy, because resistance to it is absolutely standard. Think of when you watch a world-class tennis match on TV. The player about to receive the serve doesn't stand still; they dance from side to side on their toes, keeping their options open so they can dart in the right direction once the ball comes their way. This is the mentality we're trying to create in our businesses — a situation in which people are mentally and emotionally on their toes so they can cope with and embrace change. And that's an uncomfortable state to be in; it's no wonder it's difficult to persuade everyone to adopt it.

Conclusion

I wouldn't blame you if you were feeling a little discouraged by now. This isn't my intention but it's important you understand the reasons why HR finds it so hard to change the way things are done. In my workshops I talk with many HR Managers who are trying to make things better in their companies, only to feel like giving up in despair when they encounter what seems like insurmountable resistance. When I go through what makes change such a challenge, ironically this makes it less daunting for them. They come to realise pretty much every organisation finds it difficult to shift away from the established norm. If it was easy, it would be easy!

Having said that, the situation is far from being all doom and gloom because there are ways to create transformation that are more effective and natural than what you've probably tried so far. They involve moving away from the top-down, universal roll-out approach beloved of HR change programmes, in which you attempt to persuade people to alter by offering them rational arguments and statistics. Instead, they require you to take fresh perspectives into account, in a way that's radically new in comparison to what you're used to.[14] In other words, your standard approach to change needs to... well, change.

---

[14] This is a brilliant summary of what goes wrong in traditional change management programmes: https://www.psycholgytoday.com/blog/wired-success/201411/why-change-management-fails

Action point

- Your next step is to turn to your workbook and ask yourself the key reasons for HR change being so difficult in your organisation. Go through the causes I've given you here, and note down the top three that resonate with you most. Maybe you can think of more. There's no need to worry about what you're going to do about them yet, because in the next section I'm going to help you with how you get your own HR team ready for change. Download your free workbook here: https://disruptivehr.com/thehrchangetoolkitworkbook.

Quick recap

- Persuading people to change what they've been doing for years is hard. There are several reasons for this:
  - people respond differently to reasons for change — you can't tell the same story to everyone;
  - you can't always rely on leaders to be trusted by employees when they instigate change;
  - you can't 'bribe' people to change — it's more complicated than that;
  - when change is seen to impact certain people unfairly, this demotivates everyone;
  - organisations want certainty, and effective change is messier than that;
  - leaders are usually the last people to think they need to personally change;

- o bosses don't always see the need for HR to go changing things;
- o organisations, along with HR, are steeped in a linear approach to change which doesn't work;
- o HR's traditionally parental, top-down approach to change is not effective; and
- o remaining in an agile state of constant openness to uncertainty is generally not the norm.

Section 3

Prepare Your HR Team

It's human nature to want to roll up your sleeves and plunge into changing things straightaway. Actually, if that's the way you feel I'm glad you're so fired up. But what I and my business partner, Karen Moran, see so often is HR Managers and Directors laying out ambitious plans for organisation-wide change before their own teams are ready for them. Their people don't have the skills they'll need for the challenge ahead, and just as importantly, they don't have the credibility. Then they wonder why they're not listened to by leaders around the business, or even when they are, why the pilots and processes they put in place aren't appreciated by their users. I've been there, and I don't want this to happen to you.

When I faced this problem in the past my standard re-action was to artificially create credibility for HR by bringing in a project manager from outside my team. Surely this person, with their experience in steering enormous IT programmes and their whizzy spreadsheet skills, should be ideal for the job? I was wrong. All it achieved was the disempowerment of my own team and, even worse, the creation of an HR Transformation programme that pressed all the wrong buttons. I learned that to create truly effective change there's no substitute for having an HR team with the right attitude, mindset, skills, and attributes. Because as you've just learned, change isn't a one-off job, it's a continual process of improvement. If you and your team can't take permanent ownership of it you'll be forever dependent on the expertise and credibility of others, and you'll never achieve what you want.

In this section we'll look at how you can prepare your own HR team for the changes that lie ahead. This is a vital first step and one that many HR Directors and Managers miss. First you'll learn how to build HR's credibility in your organisation, so you're more likely to be listened to. After that I'll encourage you to examine your beliefs and

assumptions about HR, because it's important to identify your starting point before you work out where you
want to go. Finally you'll have the chance to complete a
'change readiness' checklist, which will get you clear on
how prepared you and your team are for the transformation you want to implement.

As they say, change starts from within so let that be
within your own HR team first.

Build Your HR Team's Credibility

I've learned through personal experience how tough it can be to make worthwhile changes when you lack credibility within your organisation. This began with my first HR directorship at service delivery company Serco. I'd been promoted rapidly from a non-HR role, and while I was delighted with the move up it meant that overnight I was catapulted from having minimal formal HR experience to being responsible for 60,000 staff in a company with a £3 billion turnover. When I look back on it I can see I wasn't fully equipped for the job and it's not surprising I had a credibility issue, but at the time I just thought if the board hadn't believed in me they wouldn't have given me the promotion in the first place. You'll therefore not be surprised to learn that people around the business weren't too ready to take my advice. When I tried to make my views known the response was often, 'Well, how would she know anything about that? She hasn't got the experience.'

It was fascinatingly different when I subsequently moved to legal firm Eversheds as HR Director. Because the people there only knew me at that level, my authority was a given and gave me the ready ears of leaders around the business — even though I was saying many of the same things as I'd said at Serco. It made me realise how much internal promotion can affect a person's credibility. When I left Eversheds to become Group HR Director of the BBC I faced a different credibility problem. In this new environment creative content makers and producers were the ones with influence, and everyone in support functions such as HR, Legal, and Finance found their voices mattered less. This is a common issue in industries in which operators have a strong platform.

I only tell you this to illustrate that I know how frustrating and demoralising it can be not to have credibility in your company, and what a barrier it is to creating change. If you want to make a difference, the first step is therefore to tackle the HR authority issue head on.

The credibility challenges for HR

There are six main credibility issues from which HR suffers most.

The female dominance of HR

I debated with myself whether or not to include this concern, because the last thing I want is to cause controversy for the sake of it. But if I don't mention it, it will be the elephant in the room. Not long ago I was asked to speak to a group of highly talented, aspiring HR people at a networking event. As I walked into the room all I could hear were female voices. Chatting with the young women who came up to me, I found myself wondering, 'Would I take advice from her if I were a 50-year-old male Finance Director?' The fact is there are significantly higher numbers of women than men in HR, and this unfortunately affects the way people on the outside see the function. It's not only about external perceptions, either. Men tend to have more confidence in projecting their ideas than women and therefore get listened to more readily. Is this fair? Of course not. As a female HR professional myself this bias frustrates me as much as I'm sure it does you, and a significant reason for me writing this book is to give HR Managers the tools to empower themselves. But I have to argue that for this reason, and others, it's my belief that having a blend of genders in HR teams is important so as to redress the balance. We have to work even harder at building credibility because of that gap.

Our authority isn't automatically recognised

We often think that because we're professionals, this gives us automatic authority. But in reality, our leaders don't tend to value our qualifications. This seems unfair when we've worked so hard to put those letters after our names, but the honest truth is that to most people the HR profession isn't a 'thing'. What matters to them instead is whether we share their passion for what they do and are focused on enabling them to do it. If we can let go of our old ideas and become braver and more creative, this is what will give us more authority.

Another way we've tried to fill the credibility gap through status has been by seeking a seat at the boardroom table. There must be hundreds of articles online about how we can improve our influence by doing this, and many of us waste huge amounts of time trying to gain an increase in positional power rather than addressing the main reason we haven't got it already: our lack of credibility. What's more, I've been on boards and I've not been on boards, and it didn't make a huge difference to the amount of influence I was able to wield. I discovered that the meetings and activities that took place outside of the monthly board gatherings were the ones at which the most significant decisions were made.

We've been parental in our approach for so long

Given that we've spent much of our time acting either as a nursemaid or as the compliance police, it's understandable we lack credibility. In fact, 60 to 70 percent of HR time has been shown to be spent on transactional tasks rather than on those that add transformational value.[15] This shows a lack of vision, which doesn't help us when we want to be listened to.

Our siloed structures

Even though Dave Ulrich has progressed in his thinking in recent years, most of us still practise his old-style, three-pronged approach to HR.[16] In fact, 82 percent of organisations that have undergone HR transformations in the past 10 years have relied on his type of reasoning. This creates silos in our working, blocking the emergence of a joined-up perspective for HR service delivery.

HR skills gaps

Ironically, given our emphasis on qualifications, we have major skills gaps in HR. A lack of digital expertise is a key example of this, and I'll go into the topic of skills in more detail in the next chapter.

We need to admit we've made mistakes

This brings me to the final issue, which is that in order to improve HR's credibility we need to admit we've been getting things wrong for many years by not treating employees as adults, consumers, and human beings. When I talk to HR Managers I find they're reluctant to acknowledge this; they think if they admit their mistakes this will damage their image. Actually, the opposite is true. If we come clean about them we'll have the opportunity to

---

[15] https://hrtrendinstitute.com/2016/01/04/6-major-trends-in-hr-shared-service-organizations

[16] https://www.orion-partners.com/wp-content/uploads/Orion_UlrichSurveyDocument_FINAL_AMENDv2.pdf

show we've listened to the disgruntled voices around us, and this opens up a space for us to explain what we want to do differently. In any case, let's face it, we won't be telling people anything they don't already know; many managers are avid readers of new-style leadership articles in publications such as the *Harvard Business Review* and *Forbes Magazine*, and can see companies need to change. If we don't start from a place of 'mea culpa' we'll continue to be viewed as the followers and not the drivers of this change.

It's tough to acknowledge we've made mistakes. I've been guilty of defending HR approaches that were clearly not working, either because I was following accepted wisdom or didn't want to look bad. But this self-preserving attitude had the opposite effect to the one I wanted, as I discovered when I experimented with admitting what I'd been doing wrong. While defending processes about which I had my doubts made me appear disingenuous, showing humility and admitting my faults helped me to build trust. I found myself being listened to, and this gave me the opportunity to present the new insights I'd developed and to start engaging people with my ideas.

There's another excellent reason for admitting our mistakes, which is that helping our own HR teams to critically reflect on them is the only way of making sure they don't repeat them. It's unlikely they've been encouraged to challenge the processes they've been blindly implementing for years; on the contrary, they've probably been rewarded for gaining compliance with them.

To sum up, I often see HR Directors and Managers trying to leapfrog the self-examination part of the process and move straight into doing things differently, and it doesn't work. We need the right skills, attitudes, and mindsets in place so we can build great relationships around our businesses. In other words, if we want respect we have to earn it by developing our HR teams, and the next three chapters will go through how to achieve that. Let's agree your approach this time will be different. Are your people willing to admit they — and you — have been getting it wrong? Do they have a genuine desire to change? Because lasting transformation can only start from within.

Action point

- In your workbook, rate your own HR team's credibility from one to five according to each of these three areas. You can download your workbook here: https://disruptivehr.com/thehrchangetoolkitworkbook.

Quick recap

- A lack of HR credibility is a key barrier to changing an organisation.

- We in HR struggle with credibility because we:

  o   are female-dominated;

  o   are over-reliant on a status that doesn't exist;

  o   have been parental in our approach for too long;

  o   are organised in siloes;

  o   lack key skills; and

  o   haven't admitted our mistakes.

- Increased credibility starts with building your HR team's skills, mindsets, and attitudes so that they're ready for the long-term challenge ahead.

Review Your Team's Beliefs and Skills

Here's a question for you: what do you see as the role of HR? It's a deceptively simple query, but your answer to it will be revealing. When I ask this of the HR Managers I meet they usually leap into a parenting-style response: 'We're here to make sure the right people are in place at the right time, and to help them feel engaged and positive.' In other words, they see their main remit as creating policies and procedures they nursemaid employees through following, and ensuring those who don't comply are forced to.

Is that the way you see HR too? If so you may feel you should own all the company 'people processes', and you're not alone. This is why, for instance, we collate the data from the employee engagement survey instead of sending it straight to line managers, because we don't think they'll use it wisely. So much of what HR does in terms of its compliance role is based on the notion that it doesn't trust people to behave well; it's amazing how many HR Managers assume leaders and line managers aren't capable of managing. This is partly because we've witnessed so much poor management in the past, but it doesn't mean the lowest common denominator should always prevail. Our starting point could be that those managers might not be doing a good job today, but that the majority are capable of improving.

As a leader in HR who wants things to change, it's worth checking the underpinning beliefs of your team. Knowing their starting point is important because otherwise you won't be able to prepare them for what's going to shift. Do they believe everyone in the business comes to work to do a decent job, or do they assume a large proportion will try to get away with the bare minimum or even damage the company in some way? Do they see employees as individuals with their own personal motivations, or as a homogeneous lump? These are important questions.

Where does your value come from?

To gauge your people's starting point, it's worth finding out how your team members gain a sense of their own value; this might be different from what you assume. Some HR professionals derive their worth from keeping the company safe, which leads them to create multiple procedures. The smarter HR people I've worked with, however, recognise they want to be valued for more than that — for working strategically to transform their businesses. They yearn to affect the company culture and the relationship dynamics within it, and see their role as *creating the conditions* in which the business can grow, be more innovative, and achieve its goals. This distinction is an important one, because if your team assumes its job is to deliver a service, they'll focus on making that service more efficient and cost effective. But if they assume it's to enable people to work collaboratively, and be innovative and agile, their mindset will be completely different. If you've got a significant proportion of your team who are the former, you'll need to work out what to do about it.

This becomes clearer when we take a look at the evolution of HR as a profession. Picture the 'ascent of man' chart, which I'm sure you've seen many times. On the left-hand side is the personnel evolution many years ago, which was based on HR playing the role of a transactional service provider. We handled pay queries, sorted out problems, and generally helped jolly things along. As we matured and were told we were now strategic business partners, we saw the advent of developments such as the HR Business Partner, who served the business homogeneously rather than catering for individual employees' needs. This led us primarily to do leaders' bidding, which could lead to conflicts of interest (I'm sure you've experienced disciplinary hearings in which you've walked in with the line manager and left the team member to the union rep). My feeling is we're now in the middle of a third evolution, which is that while there's still a level of partisanship to our relationships with people, we're also starting to create the conditions in which they can do their best work.

The skills you need in your HR team

Recently an HR guru identified 125 competencies every HR person should have. I don't know about you, but that makes me want to give up right now! Of course we need HR people with a solid understanding of certain elements of the job such as employment law, but they need to be much more than process experts with 125 ticks to their name. I'd like to focus on the skills we need to make change happen and how well-equipped HR teams are to deliver it. Here are the skills I'd be looking for if I was putting together an HR team today.

Consumer marketing skills

We'll look at this in more detail later on, but if you have people in your team who understand the basic techniques of gathering customer insights, motivating buying behaviours, and getting your messages across in an effective way, you've got a fantastic asset. The HR experts I meet who have a marketing background think differently from the norm and bring a useful set of perspectives.

Human behavioural science skills

This is an area we'll come back to again and again in this book, so I won't go into it further now. However, if you don't have anyone who has qualifications or experience in psychology or how people think and behave, you need to look at how you can bring this in.

Digital and social media skills

Any HR solution for the future needs to have a digital component, or at least to start with a digital mindset, because digital brings with it not only the relevant technology but also taps into how people behave. It dictates how we gather information, how we think, and how we communicate with one another. If you have team members who understand the concepts behind how modern technology works (that it delivers information to us on a mobile device when and how we need it, in bite-sized chunks) you're all set. This doesn't mean you need a bunch of tech whizzes, but if you haven't got someone who understands that successful change isn't just about delivery via technology, but about the very nature of how we learn and communicate today, it's an issue.

Generic skills and attributes

I'm inspired by the work that drinks company Red Bull have done in this field. They teamed up with psychology professors from University College London and Columbia University New York to discover what attributes contribute to an employee's success over time. They came up with four:

- connections (managing relationships);
- thinking (reasoning and problem solving);
- creativity (original and innovative thinking); and
- drive (level of ambition).

I would say these are also relevant for any HR team. I'm not usually a fan of psychometric tests but this one seems credible to me and is free to use; you'll find it at www.wingfinder.com/science. It's worth asking yourself if you have people in your team who show evidence of possessing most of these attributes, even if not all four, because they need to be represented across your team in some way.

Action point

- Go through these core skills and allocate them (if you can) to the members of your HR team. Record the names and skills in your workbook, which you can download here: https://disruptivehr.com/thehrchangetoolkitworkbook.

Quick recap

- Do you and your team see the role of HR as a parental or as an enabling one?

- Where does your team's sense of value come from? As people who check the right things are done, or as people who help employees to become more innovative, agile, and productive?

- Your HR team members need to have basic HR skills, but also the ability to manage relationships, problem solve, be creative, and have ambition and resilience.

- If you and your team are to create meaningful change, your underpinning beliefs and skill set have to be used in such a way that they are assets rather than hindrances.

Get Rid of 'HR Speak'

Every profession develops its own language, and we're no different in HR.[17] However, I see the prevalence of 'HR speak' as part of our problem with instigating change because it has such a negative impact on our credibility. It doesn't make sense to our internal customers, confusing and alienating them, and it throws up a communication barrier. Jargon doesn't make us seem more important, it makes us seem *self*-important. What's more, if we're honest we don't always know what we mean ourselves when we come out with some of our descriptions and euphemisms. 'Talent acquisition strategies', 'human capital', 'PDRs', 'HR Transformation' — let's have the confidence to use language that creates rapport instead.

With this in mind, here's a tongue in cheek (but with a serious undertone) tour through a rogues' gallery of HR jargon, with the hashtag #nobullshithr.

HR Transformation
When we use this in the context of enterprise-wide system implementation it doesn't transform HR, it only creates misery. So don't use it.

Talent acquisition
When did saying 'recruiting or hiring people' become defunct? Everyone knows what 'recruiting' means, so why

---

[17] Here's a great article which goes into more detail: https://www.tlnt.com/how-hr-speak-hurts-hr-and-some-hr-words-that-should-be-banned

do we feel the need to jazz it up to make ourselves seem more important?

Performance review
This is as unpleasant as it sounds.

All acronyms
PDRs, HCMs, LMSs — avoid the lot.

Career path
They don't exist anymore. They're just careers.

Probation
For criminals, not new members of staff.

Onboarding
Sounds like 'waterboarding'. Even aside from that, it's a horrible expression.

Talent management
Isn't that what HR does in any case? Why try to turn it into something special?

Compensation and benefits
Too 1970s, and it makes it seem as if our employees are claiming for something.

Competencies
Too 1980s.

Inclusion
Yet another attempt to re-brand equality and diversity. Some companies call it by another acronym — ED&I — just to really confuse everyone.

Performance improvement plan
A pseudonym for sacking.

HR Business Partner

This reveals our lack of confidence. We should be leading the people element of business divisions, not desperately trying to look as if we're partners on equal terms.

Human capital management

Another delightful way in which HR turns people into numbers.

When we in HR put people at a distance by using jargon, we find it that much harder to get them on our side, and even worse, leave ourselves open to ridicule. Let's start talking like the human beings we are.

Action point

- Take an honest look at the offending jargon you find yourself and your team using, and list the words in your workbook. Then think of other words you could use instead. You can download your workbook here: https://disruptivehr.com/thehrchangetoolkitworkbook.

Your Change Readiness Check

Just as when you take your car for a service the garage runs it through a system check to reveal any underlying issues, so it's helpful for you to take a quiz to assess the change readiness of your HR team. There are five areas to focus on and you'll find it helpful to record your answers in your workbook, which you can download here: https://disruptivehr.com/thehrchangetoolkitworkbook. Please be honest when you answer the questions; no-one needs to see the answers apart from you (unless you want to share it with your team) and you'll find it illuminating to discover how your score stacks up. Here goes...

1. **Credibility**

- Do human dimensions feature in your business discussions within your team?

- Is your team asked for strategic input by others around the business, as opposed to simply operational matters?

- Does your team feel it has a voice in your company?

- Is your team actively involved in important strategic debates and projects elsewhere in the organisation?

- Is your team seen as the 'people experts'?

2. Attitude

- Has your team acknowledged that HR must change?

- Do you and your team derive a sense of value from challenging organisational culture and conditions, rather than from only providing a service to line managers?

- Does your team believe line managers can't manage, so it has to do it for them?

- Does your team assume it has to own the company processes, so it can check they've been followed?

- Is your team interested in changing experiences rather than processes?

3. Digital, marketing, and 'human' skills

- Are you and members of your team active on social media?

- Is your team aware of the need for all HR systems to be mobile-oriented?

- Is your team up to speed with the latest apps?

- Does your team understand the implications of excellent UXD (user experience design)?

- Does your team know what the following terms mean:
  - employee insight;
  - employee segmention;
  - employer brand?

- Does your team have a genuine insight into human behaviour when it comes to change?

- Does your team have a sound understanding of the core human motivations?

- Does your team know what happens when humans respond to perceived threats?

4. Relationships

- Are you and your team passionate about what your business does?

- Does your team take time to get to know leaders well?

- Do your team members work together well, or are there issues between the business-facing team and the centres of expertise?

- Is your team engaged with coalitions of key people in different disciplines?

- Would these people be willing to focus on HR's priorities, dropping their own?

5. Resilience

- How brave is your team?

- How prepared is your team to take risks?

- Does your team feel easily swayed by naysayers?

I hope you found this helpful. My final words are to be realistic, especially if you answered in the negative to some of the resilience questions. No HR team will tick all boxes with full marks — that's impossible — but if your scores are low you'll need to factor this into your ambitions. You may need to 'recalibrate' your expectations, fill some gaps in your team, or even decide not to do anything for now until you've sorted these issues out. I find that a set of unrealistic expectations is a key cause of HR changes not working out, so it's better to plan what's possible than what will sound exciting but fail.

In the next section we'll look at how you can start to prepare your organisation for the change ahead.

Section 4

Prepare the Ground in Your Organisation

In this section you'll start to turn your attention outwards to your organisation as a whole, learning what you need to put in place before you make any changes. You'll be thinking about your messaging and audiences, and how you can tailor what you say to different groups of people. You'll also be introduced to the Scary Six: the key people you'll find it most difficult to convince of your plans. Alongside this you'll be challenged to consider who you could team up with internally to make things easier for yourself, and to discover the right changes to make so you're listened to by the people who matter. This is in aid of making sure you're embarking on activity which is grounded and aligned with both your external brand and your company's most intransigent problems, so your programme has validity and authenticity rather than being seen as change for change's sake. Once you've laid this groundwork you'll be ready to design your transformation.

This chapter therefore covers seven main areas:

- how to create the right story for change;
- pinpointing the best problems to solve;
- identifying your main objectors;
- the role your external brand plays in change;
- the people who can help you;
- how to deal with regulators; and
- the importance of your end customer.

Create Your Change Story

It was a wet and windy morning as I arrived at work three months after being appointed as HR Director of the BBC, and I took a deep breath to steady my nerves. Shortly I was to enter a room full of senior leaders and face my first major persuasion challenge. It was my big chance to convince them to work with some strategic changes I wanted to make, and I was determined not to blow it. As I approached the stage I reassured myself I'd done my groundwork; this included a brief chat with the Director General, my boss at the time. He'd advised me that to appeal to this audience of hardened ex-journalists I should ditch any 'fluffy HR nonsense' I had in mind and focus purely on data, empirical evidence, and facts. That was the way to win them over, he assured me, so I abandoned my usual story-telling approach and did exactly as he suggested.

Before I'd even made it to the halfway point of my talk I sensed a growing rustle of discontent, and well before I finished the questions started hurtling my way. Soon the leaders were in full Jeremy Paxman mode, ripping apart my data and querying every point I made. I was floored. Instead of enabling these people to open up and engage, I'd allowed them to question and challenge until the event descended into chaos. It was not my finest hour.

Every successful change starts with a story, and in this chapter I'll explain why telling the right stories in the right way will enable your vision to become a reality. This might be a new way for you to think about change communication because we in HR haven't traditionally paid much attention to the emotional power of stories. In fact, quite the opposite. Many HR people worry about not having *enough* data to convince senior executives to engage with them — and it's true: many leaders in Finance and Operations are a highly analytical, logical bunch who require the backup of figures to convince them of an argument. Yet what I want to emphasise is not that data is irrelevant, but that we afford it a higher level of importance than it merits. Even the most analytical person needs a story to feel inspired, and it's this that makes the difference;[18] stories excite our imagination and emotions and appeal to our creative side, whereas facts awake our inner cynic rather than inspiring action. Let's think about what a great change story could look like.

Drip, drip, drip

Our traditional HR approach to communicating the need for change tends to go like this: we summon a big-name futurist or management consultancy to speak about coming trends to our leadership team; we assume our leaders will be so bowled over by it they'll go away and shake things up; and then we feel disappointed — and somewhat baffled — when nothing concrete results. How many talks have you sat in recently about the gig economy, artificial intelligence, or the Internet of Things? Of course people in our organisations need to know this stuff, but throwing some top-line impacts at them as if from nowhere doesn't appear credible. The normal reaction of audiences will

---

[18] This *Harvard Business Review* article does a good job of explaining the limitations of seeing business in a purely scientific way: https://hbr.org/2017/09/management-is-much-more-than-a-science

be to assume it will affect somebody else someday, and that carrying on doing the same old job is perfectly acceptable for now.

When people don't have the chance to prepare themselves for change, and to think about the implications of it for their own situation, they won't engage with it. So before we dive into the art of storytelling I'm making this point, which I feel is important: if you drip-feed information and understanding to your managers, executives, and employees about what you want to change ahead of time, they'll be far more receptive to it when it happens. On the other hand if you suddenly appear with an urgent rationale and expect people to instantly agree with you, you'll end up feeling frustrated. Think of your drip-feeding as being like the groundwork a gardener does before he plants his seeds. You want to be sowing yours on fertile ground, increasing the desire for transformation in a fruitful way. We'll be looking at exactly how you can do that in a later chapter, but for now just factor it into your thinking.

Advice from Aristotle

Why not be a little grandiose occasionally? In looking at the elements of a good story, let's start with the ancient Greek philosopher Aristotle. In *The Art of Rhetoric* he describes a system of persuasion, and a methodology for creating compelling narratives. Its main factors are:

Ethos. This is the will and the character to change a situation. To be effective with this the author of the narrative must possess authority and authenticity. We've already looked at the credibility issue facing HR; it's clear that if you don't have an authoritative voice you'll struggle to get anyone to even believe your numbers and logic, let alone to trust your emotional narrative. Credibility is vital.

Logos. This is the logical structure of the argument. It provides a rigorous case for transforming problems into possibilities, which then turn into ideas and actions.

Pathos. This is the ability to understand your audience. Without this you won't be able to develop stories that work specifically for them.

From this you can see that to be persuasive you need enough authority to be listened to, a sound argument which you can back up with facts (note: not lead with them), and empathy with your specific audience so what you say resonates with them. As we go through what makes a compelling story, you'll see these three elements playing a continuous part.

The downside of data and logic

In HR, as in many other functions, we take pride in being passionate about data. In fact, Ernst and Young did a study[19] which found 81 percent of executives claimed data should be at the heart of all business decisions. We can add to this the continuing rise of the MBA, a management training programme with science at its core; given that 150,000 are awarded every year in the US alone, this has a significant impact on how business people see the importance of numbers and logic.

So what's wrong with data? It's that when it comes to telling a change story, it doesn't inspire us to take action — it only allows us to justify the decisions we've already

---

[19] http://www.ey.com/uk/en/services/specialty-services/big-data—becoming-an-analytics-driven-organisation-to-create-value

made (decisions which were, in reality, emotionally based in the first place). In fact, numbers actively work *against* persuading people to change because they appeal to the left side of our brain — the part that processes and analyses facts and figures. They lead us to engage with the argument on a purely intellectual level instead of winning us over in our hearts. This is why my presentation to the leaders at the BBC failed so dismally.

I'll give you a great example of how leading with data can work against us, again from my experience at the BBC. Every year we carried out an analysis of how our diversity and inclusion numbers compared to the national average. As I discussed the latest results with the head of one of our functions — a super smart guy as it happens — we got into a nit-picking debate when he claimed the way the disability data had been collected for the organisation was different to how it had been collected for the country as a whole. In the end I said, 'Look, are you saying we don't need to do anything to increase the number of staff with disabilities?'

'Oh no', he said, 'We definitely need to be more representative.' It was at that moment I realised all the data had achieved was to get in the way of positive change. Because numbers have that effect: instead of inspiring action they divert people's attention to picking holes in it.

There are other unintended consequences of over-using data. Robert Cialdini, one of the social psychologist authors of the book *Yes! 50 Scientifically Proven Ways to Be Persuasive*,[20] tells a story about the 'magnetic middle'. In an experiment 300 households agreed to have their energy use recorded, with the

---

[20] *Yes! 50 Scientifically Proven Ways to Be Persuasive*, by Noah J. Goldstein, Steve J. Martin, and Robert B. Cialdini. Profile Books, 2007, Chapter 4.

readings being posted on their front doors each week. Over the following few weeks those who'd previously been consuming more energy than their neighbours reduced their consumption — no surprise there. But those who'd been consuming *less* energy increased it by a higher percentage. This reveals human nature's tendency to gravitate to an average rate of behaviour, much in the same way that metal filings are drawn to a magnet. Relying too heavily on data to get our message across can have the reverse impact of the one we want, even though it seems like it should be a compelling way of persuading people.

And yet in HR we assume we have to talk about ROI, trends, and data in order to be taken seriously and avoid reinforcing our reputation as the pink and fluffy team. The problem is, we've overdone it. Of course we must show we know about the logic involved, but we can't ignore the fact we're talking to human beings. We more than anyone should be proud of our humanity, not deny it.

When to use data, and how

That being said, we do need to use some figures in our persuasive efforts. The problem is, when we take a close look at the data we have available to us in HR, we find it's of limited use. There are three types we typically collect. The first is our asset data, usually bolted onto the finance system. This tells us how many employees we have, where they work, and how much they cost us — much as if they were inanimate objects. It rarely gives us the insights we need and isn't even that accurate — for instance, it amazes me how many of us can't even tell our boards how many employees are in the company. The second type of data is engagement-based and comes from our increasingly discredited annual employee engagement surveys; clearly the insights we can gain from this are only as good as the questions we've asked and are merely a snapshot in time. The third type of data comes from line managers' assessments of their people, but this is flawed because of individual bias.[21] Even when combined, these data sets are not nearly sophisticated enough to provide a compelling basis for a narrative of change.

Having said that, we've got what we've got, so how do we pull together the logical facts we need to create an effective story? Our first task is to understand what works for our specific audience. For some leaders, a competitor analysis is what will make them sit up and take notice; for instance, the length of time it takes to recruit new staff in comparison with others in the sector. For others it could be based on the time wasted by current systems and processes, and the impact of these on customers. We have to find the data that works for them, and to use only *one or two key facts* to reinforce our point. This is crucial. When Deloitte wrote its well-known article in the *Harvard Business Review*[22] in which it quoted the two million annual hours spent on its performance management system, this was clearly the nugget that grabbed the attention of people in a business that sells hours. Another leading professional services firm I've worked with discovered 75 percent of its employees had received the same performance rating for the past five years; this became a catalyst for improving how it appraised its staff. So I'm not implying data can never be a driver for change, but that one or two key statistics are all you need. Think of it as 'shock and awe' data: the one fact that makes the difference.

---

[21] https://hbr.org/2015/02/most-hr-data-is-bad-data
[22] https://hbr.org/2015/04/reinventing-performance-management

Scaring people doesn't work

Leading with endless reams of data isn't the only thing that turns people off your message. The other is when we try to scare people with dire predictions of what will happen if they don't change. We in HR tend to assume that because we've presented the serious downside of keeping to the status quo (artificial intelligence eradicating half of the current jobs, for example) and backed it up with figures, people are bound to want to do something about it. What actually happens is they retreat into denial and hide behind the sofa, or simply refuse to accept that the message applies to them at all. This phenomenon is backed by many researchers and authors, including Margaret Heffernan in her book *Wilful Blindness* [23] and Robert Cialdini et al in *Yes!* [24] If you've ever felt frustrated that the scary message you're telling your company leaders is being ignored, this could explain why. Your audience might listen at first, but you're not giving them enough to work with to take the final step of making a change.

To summarise, when we in HR find we're not engaging our audiences with data we're tempted to throw frightening trends at them such as the impact of AI and the gig economy. We also produce multitudinous and pointless numbers in board reports, without creating a compelling narrative. Finally, we don't fully understand how data works with the human brain; if we're going to use it we should identify the key facts that matter to our

---

[23] *Wilful Blindness: Why We Ignore the Obvious at Our Peril*, by Margaret Heffernan. Simon & Schuster, 2012.

[24] *Yes! 50 Scientifically Proven Ways to Be Persuasive*, by Noah J. Goldstein, Steve J. Martin, and Robert B. Cialdini. Profile Books, 2007, Chapter 8.

specific audience and weave them into an impactful story when we present them. This is what we'll look at next.

Connecting with your audience's emotions

Compelling data might grab our audience's attention, but if we want to inspire action we have to find a way past the logic and appeal to their imagination and emotions as well.

After I'd had the chance to recover from my bruising encounter with those leaders at the BBC, I reflected on the people in the organisation who'd had the most impact with their presentation style. There was one trailblazer who stood head and shoulders above the rest: the hugely motivational and inspiring Greg Dyke. Sadly, he was fired as Director General in the wake of a political disagreement, but when he left his staff marched down Regent Street in London to protest. I can't think of many leaders whose departure would provoke a mass demonstration, and he's still talked about with affection to this day. Let's look at how he talked to people. His style was exceptionally anecdotal, personal, and story-based; if you were to look back on any of his speeches you'd find very few facts and figures because his strength was in appealing to his audience's imagination and creativity. Even the most left-brained, analytical person wants a good story — they get moved to tears by the latest John Lewis Christmas advert just like the rest of us. Recently I did a workshop with a group of scientific analysts in a research organisation and asked them: 'Who's the leader who most helped you to do more than you thought was possible?' Immediately their faces lit up as they recalled the colleagues who'd done just that. It goes without saying that to want to change we have to be able to imagine a different future; stories do that for us but percentages don't.

The science of storytelling

For those left-brainers who may be feeling a little left out by now, let me reassure you, storytelling is as much a science as an art. Researchers at Princeton University have found that, when we hear a story, the brains of both storyteller and listener show what they call 'brain to brain coupling'. Telling personal stories puts you in sync with your listeners, which means it's no surprise stories make up 65 percent of the most successful TED talks.[25] Feel-good hormones such as cortisol, dopamine, and oxytocin are released in the brain when we hear a gripping narrative. Cortisol assists with formulating memories, dopamine regulates our emotional responses and keeps us engaged, and oxytocin is associated with empathy, an important element in creating deeper relationships.[26] If you'd like to see a superb example of storytelling invoking these reactions watch educator Ken Robinson's famous TED talk and see how he uses anecdotes, humour, and humility to make some incredibly serious points.[27]

So how do we in HR become more confident about telling stories? It helps when we know there are some key elements to any narrative which will make crafting a story that much easier. In fact, learning to tell an inspiring

---

[25] https://www.forbes.com/sites/carminegallo/2014/02/28/how-sheryl-sandbergs-last-minute-addition-to-her-ted-talk-sparked-a-movement/#4d2d292f65c2

[26] http://www.harvardbusiness.org/blog/science-behind-art-storytelling

[27] https://www.ted.com/talks/ken_robinson_says_schools_kill_creativity

story is something everyone can do. One way to think about it is to use the archetypal 'hero's journey' narrative structure. This is a type of story which involves a hero who goes on an adventure, wins a victory in a decisive crisis, and comes home transformed. What better template for inspiring change could there be than that? Think of films like *The Hobbit, Jaws,* or even TV programmes such as *The Apprentice* — they all follow the same three (some say five) act structure which is universally appealing to our brains. Here's how it works.

Act One

The story begins with an introduction to the world of our hero and their 'fatal flaw'. Think of Frodo's timidity, for instance, or my reliance on processes and procedures in my earlier HR directorship days. What follows next is a call to adventure. This is a challenge or difficulty which the hero of the story is initially too daunted to accept (and may be what's stopping you now!). After accepting the call, however, (sometimes with the help or mentorship of another person) our hero leaves their place of comfort and strikes out into the unknown. This represents a commitment to change.

Act Two

Our hero undergoes a series of trials, which he or she overcomes with the help of people met and knowledge gained along the way. About halfway through the story our hero masters a major challenge in which their flaw is erased; they now have a new knowledge and perception of what they've set out to achieve. My turning point, for instance, was when I started to realise the accepted HR wisdom I'd gone along with for so long was deeply flawed and I then embarked on a series of challenges to it. After this 'mid-point' our hero is ready to continue their journey, this time in a homeward direction.

Act Three

Our hero is faced with further difficulties which enable them to consolidate their newfound strength and knowledge. After overcoming these they're often faced with one final, enormous hurdle which they vanquish before they return home, bringing with them what they've learned. For me this was the formation of my HR consultancy, Disruptive HR, which gave me the vehicle to share my insights with others.

You can see how inspiring this story structure is. Of course your story won't be in the Hollywood blockbuster style, but if you can think of it in three parts — introduction to the challenge, the challenge itself in which you gain vital knowledge, and the resolution — you'll find it hard to go off track. By all means use limited data in your stories, but only as a backup to the narrative you're already telling.[28] And remember, personal anecdotes which portray you in a human light are all the better.

---

[28] More advice here on how you can use data in your stories: https://hbr.org/2015/12/how-content-marketers-can-tell-better-stories-with-data?autocomplete=true

Action point

- Your next task is to use your workbook to bullet point the main elements of your own story for change. Keep it top line for now but use it as a way to start thinking about what you will tell people. You can download your workbook here: https://disruptivehr.com/thehrchangetoolkitworkbook.

Quick recap

- To inspire people to change, you need to tell a compelling story.

- First, drip-feed your story to the people you want to influence; don't expect them to accept it out of the blue.

- Aristotle's three elements of a persuasive story are helpful: ethos, logos, and pathos.

- Your story can't be based on data or logic but on appealing to human emotions.

- Nor can you base an effective change story on scary facts because people will go into denial.

- Use data sparingly to back up your arguments or as a 'shock and awe' tactic.

- Consider the structure of your overall story when you create it.

What's Your Problem?

Every impetus to change starts with the desire to solve a problem — that much is clear. What might be less obvious is that it's incredibly easy to go about solving the wrong problem. A problem can be 'wrong' in two ways:

- when it doesn't address the underlying cause of a difficulty, or

- when it's one your leaders don't care about and that you'll therefore be wasting your time trying to persuade them to solve.

Asking 'Why?'

Let's look at the first type of 'wrong problem' to begin with: one that doesn't address the underlying cause of a difficulty. What I'm talking about here is not the superficial issue — the one everyone's talking about — but the one that's caused it in the first place. This is usually so hidden nobody even realises it exists. So how do we uncover it? The most helpful approach is to ask a series of 'whys'. This has become known as the Six Sigma[29] approach (using five whys), and has also been adopted by businessman Ricardo Semler[30] (who advocates three).

---

[29] https://www.isixsigma.com/tools-templates/cause-effect/determine-root-cause-5-whys/

[30] http://transformationalpresence.org/alan-seale-blog/three-whys-in-a-row-the-radical-wisdom-of-ricardo-semler-on-business-education-and-life/

The most important aspect of this is not the number of whys, but what they help us uncover.

If our board keeps complaining that the business needs to change its approach to performance management, for instance, our first response in HR should be to ask, 'Why?' Each time we answer this question we get closer to the truth of the issue. The Q & A might go as follows:

'We need to change our approach to performance management.'
'Why?'
'Because it's not delivering.'
'Why?'
'Because it's not improving performance.'
'Why?'
'Because it's not helping the business to meet its challenges.'
'Why?'
'Because it's not focused on helping us to be more innovative and to stay ahead of the competition.'

This sheds a whole new light on the situation because we can now see the real issue is not that we need to change our performance management system, but that we're not being innovative enough. If we hadn't gone through the whys we'd have blindly created a more efficient way of assessing employees' performance, instead of turning our attention to how we could increase creativity in the organisation; in other words, we'd have achieved the exact opposite of what we set out to do. Hopefully this shows why it's so important to uncover the underlying dysfunction, rather than to smooth it over with an enhanced procedure. All that does is to hide it, creating yet more dysfunction in the process.

Focus on what matters to the business

Now we move onto the second type of 'wrong problem': one that leaders don't care about. The race for digital talent is a great example of how you can focus on the right one. Nowadays almost every company is becoming a digital business that happens to do something else — retailers, for instance, are online businesses that happen to sell merchandise. This fact has probably not escaped your leaders, who understand that the organisation needs to adapt to the digital challenge without delay. For this reason it's my experience that when HR people face barriers to change from within their companies, one lever they can always pull is the need to bring in, and retain, digital talent. Consider basing your change message on this instead of the crude one of, 'We need to transform our approach to leadership because of the changes our company is facing.'

A great example is a fashion magazine publisher I worked with. They're leaders in their field and have no problem recruiting people eager to work in their glamorous industry, even for low wages. This created an historical approach to leadership and line management somewhat lacking in best practice. Can you imagine being their HR Director and trying to persuade the board to change, when their leaders were feeling no pain with staff recruitment and retention? If you were to move into the sphere of the digital challenge, however, you'd find a more receptive audience.

The company's readers now expect their experience to come from Instagram and other social platforms as much as from print magazines, and the fashion bloggers are swiftly encroaching on the publisher's space.

No longer can it rely on making its money from prestige brands paying a fortune for an advert in the old-fashioned way, because it needs to work hand in hand with those same bloggers and micro influencers. This means throwing itself into competition with tech companies such as Google and Facebook in a bid to attract top coders and UXD experts, and here's where their problem lies. For this in-demand talent, fashion isn't necessarily the draw it is for their usual employees; these people want the perks of autonomy, agility, and a funky and flexible working environment, rather than fashion show tickets and endless free samples. Because of this pain, the publisher is now taking a fresh look at how it recruits, retains, and engages its employees. In this particular company's case I'm working with it to create a different employee value proposition on its digital side, which is also beginning to have an impact on the way its leaders think about their other employees as well.

The Fundamental Four

You can see from this that the need for a digital overhaul is every company's nemesis, but there are other areas of vulnerability you can look at too. Every organisation I work with, regardless of sector, seems to realise they need to be more

- innovative;
- productive;
- collaborative; and
- agile.

I call these the Fundamental Four. The requirement to be both more innovative and productive is self-explanatory. The need to be more collaborative comes from changes in digital technology and consumer habits, which mean internal teams have to work in a more joined-up way. And agility is essential to be responsive and flexible enough to meet customer requirements. When you root your proposal to change in one of these four areas you'll be listened to far more readily than if you make general statements about the need to shift your approach. If your business has a specific problem either in the Fundamental Four or elsewhere, use it as a lever. Exploit it. Think about how you can employ it not only to transform one area, but also as a trailblazer for others in the company.

Action point

- Use your workbook to list the top three domains of concern and dissatisfaction in your business as experienced by leaders (not necessarily by you). Use the Fundamental Four to get you started. You can download your workbook here: https://disruptivehr.com/thehrchangetoolkitworkbook.

Quick recap

- When people complain about a problem don't take it on the surface. Instead, drill down by asking why it arose in the first place and solve that issue instead.

- Digital is often the area in which leaders are most receptive to the need to change.

- The Fundamental Four vulnerabilities of any organisation are the need to be more innovative, productive, collaborative, and agile. Root your call for change in one or more of these.

The Scary Six

In our workshops with hundreds of HR professionals over the world, we focus on firing them up to do things differently. Once they're ready to take action we then ask them: 'Imagine you're going back to your business tomorrow. Who's the one person who'll be most resistant to your ideas?' At this point their excited faces fall as they picture the individual, and that colleague is always in one of the following groups of personnel.

We've covered the Fundamental Four problem areas, so let's call these the Scary Six problem people. Which group is yours in?

- **Leaders** — who you assume won't like the proposed change.

- **Line managers** — who you assume won't be capable of it even if they're interested (which they probably won't be).

- **Employees** — you're most likely to pick this group if you're in a traditional business that has a long-term child/parent relationship with HR.

- **Your own HR team** — who you reckon might not be able to cope with the change.

- **Unions** — who often have a vested interest in maintaining the status quo.

- **Regulators or your own internal compliance function** — these will loom large for you if you work in a heavily regulated industry such as financial services or health care.

The mistake we make

Picture the person or function you predict will be the most challenging to convince of the need to do things differently. How do you envisage winning them over? If the very thought of it tempts you to give up before you start, this will help you.

When we craft one set of messages about change that attempts to work for all people it's bound to fail, and yet so often that's exactly what we do. We might separate our stories for leaders, line managers, and everyone else, but typically we stick to treating people as one lump of listeners. I'm sure you've been on the receiving end of those types of communications — the ones where everyone's herded into the annual company results presentation and bored to death with the ritual dissection of figures, for instance. And you switch off because it doesn't feel relevant to you. In the same way, we don't tend to think about the different messages that each of the Scary Six will need to hear. Each of these groups has its own attitudes, experiences, fears, and motivations, and we should be taking them into account; if we're serious about crafting messages that work we need to dig deeper into their needs.

- What matters to them, both professionally and personally?

- What worries them, both professionally and personally?

- How do they like to be communicated with?

- How best should we influence them — through the excitement of a vision of the future or the motivation of fear of loss?

One of my first responsibilities at Serco, before I became HR Director there, was bidding for rail maintenance contracts. My most significant challenge was when we went for the Midland main line; if we won it we'd be responsible for managing and maintaining the track, signalling, and telecoms on the railway that runs all the way from Derby to London — a huge catch for us. The work would be carried out by around 500 railway workers who were ex-British Rail, and who were currently working for Balfour Beatty after British Rail had been privatised. To our delight we won the bid. At that point I had the bright idea of running some induction sessions for the new rail workers so they could find out more about us. It never occurred to me that perhaps I should have got to know them first. Because it turned out that while I'm the type to be motivated by anything that's new, exciting, or different, this was decidedly not the case for these guys. Here was a group of men for whom a 25-year length of service in railway engineering was a mere apprenticeship. They liked certainty and were not excited in the slightest by risk or change. Nor were they impressed by the prospect of new uniforms and vans, or more autonomy in decision making. And they were horrified at the idea of being re-organised into teams different to the ones they'd belonged to for decades. As I presented what I thought was a series of exciting changes to them in my energetic, extrovert manner, I felt my heart slowly sink as they sat there with their arms folded. It was certainly one of my less impressive moments.

We can see what happens when we don't know our audience, so how do we become more familiar with what they think and feel? This is where personality profiling tools come in handy. One I've found helpful is the DiSC® model, which tells you how people rate on the scale of dominance, influence, steadiness, and conscientious-ness.[31] We often use these tools when recruiting, but rare-ly when we're wanting to convince people to change.

Develop your personas

Now I know what you're thinking. 'I've got an organisa-tion of 10,000 people. There's no way on earth I'd be able to create an individual strategy for everyone.' And you're right, you can't, which is why I'd like to introduce you to the concept of personas. A persona is a kind of carica-ture — a set of motivations, predilections, situations, and characteristics that make up a certain type of individual. It doesn't attempt to reflect the subtlety of human nature and nor is it intended to. What it does do is give you a basis for your communications so you can try to predict what kind of messages will work for what characters.

I suggest you create four to six personas based on your most difficult to convert personalities. In the pro-cess of doing so you'll be engaging your imagination, which in itself makes it easier to envisage what kind of di-alogue will work for them. To get you started I've created my own personas for the Scary Six (actually I've included a seventh — the Finance Director) by recollecting the people I've previously worked with who represent these groups. I'll not go into the strategy for communicating with each of them as we'll do that later on, but the point here is to get you thinking about who you need to con-vince and what they're like. You'll need to identify the one thing that matters most to them so you can build your approach for each persona differently.

---

[31] https://discprofile.com/what-is-disc/overview.

Although my personas are based on real people I've named them after famous film and TV characters, so you can gain an immediate sense of what they're like. They're a bit humorous and somewhat exaggerated, but that's fine — as long as you 'get' them that's all that matters. This is an area in which you can have some fun. Bear in mind my personas will be different to yours — you'll probably find your challenges have their own characteristics.

The leader

Miranda Priestley in *The Devil Wears Prada*

Characteristics: based on a woman who was once my nemesis. Hugely bright, an amazing practitioner, and a long-term employee, she heads up a key division. She's incredibly charismatic, extremely powerful, and massively influential in the organisation.

Assumptions about HR: it's useful for transactional purposes only.

Attributes to beware of: in order to preserve her popularity with her staff she's lightning quick to blame HR if anything goes wrong. As an example, I remember one occasion when we took the decision to make staff cutbacks. This woman had sat in the meeting at which we'd ratified this decision and had agreed it was an essential, if regrettable, step. I later heard that when she came to announce this to her team her words were, 'You'll never guess what HR has done now...'

The Finance Director

Gordon Gekko in *Wall Street*

Characteristics: based on a Finance Director at one of the firms I once worked at. Back in the 1980s this guy was won over by the model of forced rank distribution, which led to the removal of the bottom 10 percent of employees. He's also convinced money matters to everyone equally, and that the most effective way to motivate people is through pay rises and financial bonuses. It's all about the data with him and he can't understand why everyone doesn't just do what they're told when he waves the numbers at them. He probably doesn't even like people much in any case.

Assumptions about HR: its role is to create systems and processes that force people to comply with company procedures. Its other use is controlling head counts and personnel costs.

Attributes to beware of: he's highly influential with the Chief Executive, ultra-smart, and sees HR only as a necessary evil.

The line manager

James Bond

Characteristics: based on a guy I once worked with. On the surface he doesn't seem to be a change resistor; he's been with the company for three years in a tech role and fancies himself as an HR expert and entrepreneur. He's read loads of books on leadership and HR, has strong views on the subject, and just wants his own personal HR team so he can get on with implementing the changes he's so excited about.

Assumptions about HR: it's slow and unresponsive to the needs of dynamic people like him and is stuck in the dark ages. It's holding him back.

Attributes to beware of: he can be extremely progressive but only as far as it benefits his team. If he's let off the leash to move at speed he can be an asset, but if he has to slow down to accommodate anyone else he can be incredibly resistant. At this point he plays the digital card: 'You don't understand. The people I'm trying to recruit want something different. We need to do our own thing. We want our own offices. We want our own terms and conditions. We want our own processes. We want, we want, we want...' If you try to involve this guy in anything universal or consistent with others he'll be a nightmare to manage.

The employee

Hermione Granger in *Harry Potter*

Characteristics: based on an amalgamation of many young women I've worked with. She's 31 years old, highly ambitious, and super smart, she's been an A grade student throughout her academic career. To her delight she's been promoted rapidly in her first few years of employment. She wants new roles. She loves differentiation. She adores bonuses.

Assumptions about HR: its function is to give her regular, positive feedback in the form of succession planning grids, leadership courses, and favourable performance ratings.

Attributes to beware of: beneath her confident exterior she's incredibly needy, maintaining her self-esteem by relying on the gold stars bestowed by traditional HR high potential programmes. This leads her to be brittle and non-collaborative when pushed.

The HR team member

Marge Simpson in *The Simpsons*

Characteristics: based on one of my former team members, who was a wonderful person. She's been with the company for 30 years and is in her mid-50s. Devoted to her business leader, she's as much admired by him as he is by her. She's extremely process-oriented, loves to be needed, is compliant and proud of it, and is always so, so busy. She just wants to sort out people's problems, which she does extremely thoroughly.

Assumptions about HR: there's no need to do things differently. Looking after people is what HR is all about and is where the job satisfaction lies.

Attributes to beware of: if there's a new approach you want to roll out she won't outright oppose it but will resort instead to passive-aggressive resistance by not fully co-operating. To compound this her business manager thinks the sun shines out of her backside because she takes so much work off his plate, so why would he support any change?

The union representative

Grug the dad in *The Croods*

Characteristics: based on a union guy I once worked with. He's fair minded and traditional but only interested in preserving the status quo for his members, who are on gold-plated benefits due to their length of service. As soon as he feels this is threatened he flies off the handle.

Assumptions about HR: if you give them an inch they'll take a mile. Also, they should stick to the same processes and procedures for all to keep things fair.

Attributes to beware of: he sees everything in terms of transactional deals, so if HR wants to introduce more movement of talent around the organisation he'll jump on that as an opportunity to ask for increased benefits. He has no interest in the differing needs of millennials or in new ways of doing things. If you advocate for segmenting the employee-base to cater for people's differing needs, for instance, he'll accuse HR of introducing inequality through the back door.

The internal auditor

Sir Humphrey Appleby in *Yes Minister*

Characteristics: based on a guy I once worked with who was a 42-year-old internal auditor. Fiercely protective of his company, he's incredibly loyal and has worked there for 18 years. His sole rationale is to make sure reputational and financial risks are minimised, which leads him to be obsessed with systems and processes.

Assumptions about HR: its role is to manage and maintain staff records to prove compliance with regulatory standards.

Attributes to beware of: he doesn't care whether the current performance management conversations are delivering value, he's more concerned about proving they've taken place. The notion HR might move away from having central registers of compliance, by dismantling cumbersome learning management systems and moving to a more agile and learner-driven approach, brings him out in a cold sweat.

Action point

- In your workbook create your own key 'Scary Six' personas (you don't need to have all six). What are their main characteristics, assumptions about HR, and attributes to beware of? Don't feel you have to stick to the format I've given you — feel free to give your imagination and creativity the space it needs to come up with some juicy characters. It's helpful to involve your team in this — imagine what fun you could have together! You can download your workbook here: https://disruptivehr.com/thehrchangetoolkitworkbook.

Quick recap

- When it comes to the most difficult character you'll have to persuade there are six main types: leaders, line managers, employees, your own HR team, unions, and regulators.

- In order to be listened to you'll need to ensure your messages speak to the concerns and desires of each group individually.

- Creating personas for your main 'problem people' is a great way of tapping into their psychology so you can communicate effectively with them.

Align HR with Your External Brand

Think about the last time you went clothes shopping. If you're over the age of 30 I'm guessing you didn't pay a visit to a store like Abercrombie & Fitch, but if you had, your experience would have been horrible. The stores are nightclub dark, banging music fills the air, and the assistants wander around in strange outfits. You can't hear, you can't see, and you find yourself muttering phrases like, 'Why does it have to be so *loud* in here?' If you were in their target market, however, you'd be delighted by the teenage atmosphere keeping the old fogies out. As another example, if you visit an Apple store you can't fail to be impressed with the company's attention to technical detail. There's no obvious cash desk, with the staff wielding portable payment devices instead. The beautiful store layout and design, along with the iconic buildings in which their shops are often sited, are superbly aligned with the consumer brand.

What these two retailers have in common is that they're completely clear on what their brands stand for, and they translate that into what marketers call 'moments of truth'. These can be broken down into the different stages of the customer journey, from the moment their customers enter the door, to the interactions they have with staff during their visit, right through to how any after-care complaints are handled. Smart companies ensure these customer experiences are a reflection of, and support, their brand, and understand how they create a unified experience of it. This doesn't happen by accident: it's the result of an endless interplay between merchandisers, buyers, product creators, staff trainers, and shop designers. Only recently has this started to include HR.

How alignment works (or doesn't)

When the external experience our customers have of our company aligns with the internal experience our employees have of it, a powerful link is forged. And when the messages our staff give out to our customers — whether overt or subliminal — reinforce the impression our CEO wants to create, we've got marketing dynamite. This isn't a new concept for HR, but how many of us have translated our brand's moments of truth into those of our employees? They're with us all week not just for an hour on a Saturday afternoon, which means we have more opportunity to get the moments right and, of course, to get them badly wrong. Time and again, we inadvertently undermine our brands by giving our employees experiences that contradict our brand promise. This is a problem, because it's these same employees we trust to deliver that promise every day. Customers and the media are now so quick to share their experiences of a brand, we can't create one proposition for customers and another for employees — it just doesn't work anymore.

There are many ways in which the value statements a company makes to its customers aren't supported by HR practices. I'll give an example from my days at the BBC. As you're probably aware, the BBC brand is based on excellence in creativity, impartiality, and fairness; if you've watched standout shows like *Blue Planet* you can see how they work so well together. Because of this we never had any difficulty in recruiting people; we fielded hundreds of thousands of applications a year. But when our new employees started on their first day they soon realised the inside of the organisation was markedly different to what they'd been led to expect. Endless form filling, paternalistic checks, and bureaucratic hoop-jumping were the norm. And once that recruit had been there long enough to have a new idea, it would have to be approved by several levels of seniority. It certainly didn't seem to them as if they were working in a creative organisation.

Let's see some other examples of how this plays out if you're an employee. There's the fast-moving, dynamic tech business that sends wads of strictly worded employment policies to you before you join. There's the telecoms company whose brand promise is about connecting families and friends, and yet on your first day you get shown straight to the cubicle in which you're expected to work in isolation. There's the healthcare organisation that builds its brand around having a team approach, yet rewards its staff with individual bonuses. There's the insurance company that promises peace of mind to its customers, but lets redundancies drag on for months. And there's the high street retail store you can 'trust', but forces you to clock in every day. These are all examples of a cognitive dissonance between what a consumer brand says, and the experience of its employees.

Virgin does this differently.[32] I know from having worked with the company that it's got a marketing approach to its employees, and that it tries hard to reflect its external brand internally. For instance, it created 'Virgin

---

[32] http://www.synergycreative.co.uk/gossip/aligning-corporate-and-employer-brands-how-does-virgin-do-it

Tribe'.[33] This is a discount site on Virgin brands for employees, which has also become a strategic brand asset across the group. In addition to discounts, it's used to share stories and to connect the entire Virgin employee community.

Whole Foods Market is another example of close brand alignment, and it's been ranked among Fortune Magazine's top 100 companies to work in for the past 17 years. One of its values is 'We support team member excellence and happiness', and a way it achieves this is by offering all employees stock options after 6,000 hours of service, regardless of rank. What's more, only teams have the power to approve new hires for full-time posts, not individual managers. Store leaders screen candidates and recommend them for a job on a specific team, but two thirds of the team have to vote for them to stay after their 30-day trial period. This is a brilliant generator of trust, which is reinforced by each store having an open book listing the previous year's salary and bonus for all employees — by name. You can see how these HR policies support the brand proposition of excellence and happiness.

Airbnb has a brand promise that centres on 'belonging' and feeling at home.[34] It does many things to reinforce this internally. One is that every employee can create their own page on its intranet and within reason can put what they like on there. They can talk about their passions, what they enjoy, and who they think themselves to be. Through this they're helping others to get to know

---

[33] http://www.synergycreative.co.uk/gossip/aligning-corporate-and-employer-brands-how-does-virgin-do-it

[34] You can see more interesting examples of how they achieve this here: https://www.forbes.com/sites/jeannemeister/2015/07/21/the-future-of-work-airbnb-chro-becomes-chief-employee-experinece-officer/2/#620d5d575535

them, thereby creating a feeling of acceptance and belonging. The company also takes this one step further. When it has a conference at its base in California, instead of putting delegates from outside the area in a hotel, they're hosted by local employees in their homes. Because that's what the brand ethos is about.[35]

Ask yourself: what's the promise you make to your customers and is this reflected in your employees' experiences? Or are you guilty of creating a disconnect between the two? I appreciate it's generally easier to understand your brand proposition if you sell to consumers rather than to other businesses but take a stab at describing it. What do you stand for? What experiences do you promise? Then work through your employee moments of truth. Where do elements of your employee experience contradict your external brand? Where do they align? And where are they neutral? Because it's the lack of congruity that will be impacting your engagement levels, stopping people doing their best work, and reducing your employee advocacy. When done badly it can lead to people feeling disappointed and leaving, and when done well it can increase sales, ease recruitment, and even transform your business.

---

[35] https://blog.cultureamp.com/how-airbnb-is-building-its-culture-through-belonging

Action point

- Your findings will give you a focus for action, which you can record in your workbook. You can download it here: https://disruptivehr.com/thehrchangetoolkitworkbook.

Quick recap

- Successful brands understand why creating consistent moments of truth for their customers is so essential.

- The experience of employees in many companies is not consistent with the external brand, leading to a cognitive dissonance between the two.

- When consumer brand and employee experience are aligned, this adds to the company's strength.

- HR needs to work harder to bring the two together.

Build Useful Coalitions

No-one has all the skills they need to make change happen — it's not humanly possible. You're going to need allies in the camp. Some of the world's most enduring innovations have come through combining differing talents, resources, and outlooks. Who could doubt the united power of Lennon and McCartney, Larry Page and Sergey Brin, or Ben Cohen and Jerry Greenfield?

Traditionally HR has buddied up with Finance when it's wanted to make an impact, but in my view that's incredibly limiting. We've seen how focusing purely on numbers and statistics is harming our work, so let's look further afield for people who can help us to create change. Who can you turn to for inspiration and support in your mission? You'll not be surprised, given the last chapter's emphasis on aligning HR with your external brand, that it's your colleagues in Marketing who should be your first port of call. Marketing people are experienced practitioners of the art of customer research and segmentation, which is vital for developing your understanding of your employee base. They're also geniuses at communication, especially when it comes to motivating and persuading people. Virgin Trains HR, for instance, teamed up with its customer insight team to generate research into the employee base, and with its branding team created personalised communications for its staff.

There's also some interesting research[36] into how well the collaboration between HR and Marketing can work, where it does exist. The conclusion is that for integration to be successful both parties need to be aligned with one another. But when the research subjects were asked how well this was happening both departments acknowledged there was room for improvement; HR gave Marketing three out of five for collaboration, with Marketing's score at 3.5. Don't let this put you off, though. These scores reflect the continuing evolution of this relationship which is still in its early stages in most businesses; the roles, accountability, and effectiveness of each aren't yet clear.

There are other options for collaboration, although they're less obvious. Researcher and writer Jacob Morgan[37] has examined the employee experience and has completed, in my opinion, the most forward-thinking and comprehensive work available on how we can see it. His view is that it's formed of three things: the company culture, the tools people have to do their jobs, and the physical working environment. The culture is obviously the area HR can have the biggest impact on, which is what this book's all about. Providing the tools to do the job is generally IT's domain — we all know how frustrating it is when we can't get on our internal WhatsApp group because they've put a block on it, for instance. Plus, IT can impact on working culture in more proactive ways, such as by implementing AI driven chatbots to remove the distraction of basic HR email requests.[38] In terms of the working environment it's our facilities and procurement

---

[36] https://omobono.com/application/files/1014/6944/7186/6282_WWW2016_Report_AW_WEB_CP.pdf

[37] You can read more about his thoughts here: https://thefutureorganization.com/category/employee-experience

[38] https://omobono.com/insights/blog/hr-and-technology

functions that control this, and we often underestimate their importance. We in HR don't tend to have much to do with these other functions until we have an outsourcing arrangement for HR advisory services to put in place, or we buy an IT system for HR. But if you think about it, with the increase in the gig economy and the freelancers and contractors that come with it, having an excellent relationship with our procurement and IT teams makes a lot of sense.

Then there's the product design function. How can the people there help us? Later on we'll look more closely at what we can learn from product design when we launch and improve our services. Even the simple act of going to talk to these people from around the business is a bridge-building exercise. We can not only find out how they can help us but also how well (or otherwise) we're helping them right now.

Action point

- Your next task is to go to your workbook and rate your relationships with these key business areas: Marketing, IT, Procurement, Facilities, and Product Design. Next, prioritise the one you're going to build a closer relationship with first and start to think about how you might do that. You can download your workbook here: https://disruptivehr.com/thehrchangetoolkitworkbook.

Quick recap

- Building coalitions with key functions in your business is essential if you want to create lasting change.

- Focus your efforts on Marketing, IT, Procurement, Facilities, and Product Design rather than on the traditional partner of Finance.

Get Regulators on Your Side

Going back to our Scary Six objectors to HR change, you'll remember regulators were one of them, and depending on your industry they may even be your most serious concern. HR Managers in financial services, health care, education, and the public sector frequently find themselves struggling with regulators when they want to do away with procedures. These regulators love to focus on inputs from HR, so they insist on job descriptions for each part of your organisation, training records, and performance ratings for everybody. I often hear HR people say these auditors are an insurmountable barrier to change, and being honest, in some cases I think they might be. But as with so many challenges when it comes to achieving what you want, this is less often the case than you assume. If you feel regulators are preventing you from doing interesting, new, fresh, and innovative things, don't just accept it. There's a two-step process to approaching the problem.

1. **Digest and interrogate the detail by getting to know your regulatory or quality frameworks in depth.** There are no short cuts to this I'm afraid, but there's huge value in what you unearth. The next time you suggest changing something and your internal auditor responds with, 'Oh, the regulator won't allow you to do that,' look instead at what *outcome* that regulator is trying to guarantee. Often what they want to see is that HR is ensuring the right skills are in place, it's complying with

108 The HR Change Toolkit

the law, and that there's clarity around responsibilities. These are all worthy things to aim for, but the problem comes with how you're expected to prove them. Does the regulation specifically ask for the processes themselves to be completed, or is it simply the supposed outcomes of those processes it's interested in? In other words, does it require you to have a learning management system that documents every qualification and course taken, or is it more concerned with knowing whether or not your employees have the right skills and qualifications for their jobs? If it's the latter, it's your task to find more creative ways of giving them what they want.

As an example of this, let's look at the Financial Conduct Authority training and competence standards.[39] What's interesting is that it gives HR some leeway in proving employee competence: 'Firms decide which methods to use when assessing employee competence. We define competence as having the skills, knowledge and expertise needed to discharge the responsibilities of an employee's role.' This is a pretty broad requirement — there's nothing in here about carrying out performance management assessments, skills gap analysis, or competency frameworks — but unless you were to interrogate it you wouldn't know.

2. **Embark on a long-term education project.** If your regulators do require these processes, then sadly you're going to have to embark on a long-term education process with them so they eventually

---

[39] https://www.fca.org.uk/firms/training-competence

understand processes don't necessarily guarantee the outcomes they're looking for. Before you roll your eyes, bear in mind that, as a profession, HR has done an excellent job of encouraging auditors and regulators to buy into the idea that these processes work, which means unravelling the situation will take some doing. Any regulator who's asked to give up a standard or remove a compliance factor will be reluctant to do so because you're asking them to try something new. For this reason it's helpful to have some worked-through solutions to offer them right from the beginning, so they can see you've thought about the implications of change.

Action point

- In your workbook list the regulators you have to satisfy (assuming you have them). Your next task is to look into the detail of their requirements and work out which of these two approaches you will take. You can download your workbook here: https://disruptivehr.com/thehrchangetoolkitworkbook.

Quick recap

- If you have regulators to satisfy, first interrogate the detail in their policies to define whether it's processes or outcomes they're interested in.

- If it's the latter, work with them to find more creative ways to satisfy their needs.

- If it's the former, you'll need to embark on a long-term education project.

Focus on Your End Customer

In HR we understandably focus on the internal workings of our organisations, but let's not forget the ultimate reason we do this: to improve our product or service for our end customers. This means there has to be a connection between the changes we ask people to make and the customers we serve at the end of the process. In fact, most people in the organisation will be more persuaded by the desire to do a good job for the latter, than they will be by the need to change the way they do things internally 'for the sake of it'.

I don't think we take this view often enough in HR — we don't look at the 'why'. For instance, when BBC North was created, the team in that area did an amazing job of relating everything back to the audiences in North West England where they were situated. The creation of MediaCity in Salford was one of the most impressive and successful change programmes I've ever seen, and at the heart of it was the need to connect with the regional audience. The way they did it was to create messaging around the need for change which was clear and indisputable, with the senior team aligned behind it. All changes which affected people had an ultimate goal, and if they didn't help the BBC connect with and appeal to viewers and listeners in the region they weren't considered a priority. Whether it be improvements to technology, employee behaviours, or even the buildings they worked in, every-thing came back to the North West.

You can see from this how a focus on your end cus-tomer can be helpful when introducing new approaches, but it can also be of benefit when you want to get rid of legacy policies and processes that don't add value. If you ask your people which are the ones that most get in the way of you providing a great service to customers, it quickly becomes clear where you're wasting your time and energies. And finally, if you keep asking yourself how your proposed changes benefit your end customer you'll create a discipline that helps to bring your leaders and employees on board, because you all share this end goal.

Section 5

Design Your Change

Now you've prepared your HR team and thought about how you're going to get people in your organisation onside, we come to how you're going to shape your change. Here's where it gets exciting, because designing your transformation is the moment when you start to envisage what it will look like. Who will use it? What will they like best about it? And how will it make work easier, more innovative, and more productive for everyone?

We'll start with why implementing a traditional, system-based HR transformation project isn't the answer (which will be a relief, I promise you), and also why a marketing approach to segmenting and targeting your audience is so crucial. Then we'll examine how learning from Product Design will help you create credible and user-friendly services, as well as ones that are less stressful and time-consuming to develop than you'd expect. In the process you'll start to take on an agile, product-related mindset, which will stand you in good stead when it comes to putting your ideas into practice. It's a radical move away from how HR tends to do things now, but it will open your eyes to a fresh and — just as importantly — more effective way to go about transformation.

This section therefore covers three main areas:

- HR transformations and why they don't work;
- getting clear on who you're creating your change for; and
- learning to think like an agile product designer in order to create useful change.

Don't Embark on HR Transformation

It may seem strange to start a chapter in a book about how to change HR, by saying HR transformations don't work. However, I'm referring to HR Transformation with a capital 'T': the one that for most HR professionals is synonymous with change. In other words, the implementation of a brand new, global HR IT system. Unfortunately, the painful truth is that this type of HR Transformation rarely transforms HR, and here's why.

Every HR transformation programme I've ever had the misfortune or stupidity to get involved with has started with someone in Finance asking my team to do a benchmarking exercise with the aim of saving money. I duly obliged, comparing staffing ratios, costs per employee, comparative investment in learning, and other factors. There was a loud tutting around the board table as HR's efficiency was examined, making us appear to be too expensive, overly resourced and, plainly, useless. Large, powerful consultancy firms, with equally megalithic systems to sell, would then be invited to explain how we could become more efficient and cost effective if only we would invest in their platforms. A feasibility study would ensue, which showed we could centralise transactional tasks, standardise and automate our core processes, and make huge savings in HR staff to boot. These economies were almost always the driving force behind the change. Later on, however, we'd start to see additional 'benefits'. We'd enthuse about how much easier the manual processes the system replaced would now be for staff around the business to work with. How managers would relish having their organisation charts at their fingertips, we imagined. How they'd love poring over their people data and analytics. How much fun they'd have with their automated succession planning grids. The world would be their oyster!

You can see where this evangelistic zeal came from, because the idea behind these systems is they achieve an HR holy trinity: managers around the business owning processes, employees being able to service their day-to-day requirements themselves, and HR finally being able to standardise procedures from the centre. It's the third part I'm embarrassed to say I loved the most. Instead of each department of the business having its own approach to talent management, for instance, it was co-ordinated centrally. It was parental HR nirvana, and unfortunately still is.

What's not to like? Well, a company called TI People has done some interesting research and has discovered eight out of ten large companies run these programmes, with an average spend of $10 million per year among those in the Fortune 500. And yet less than 20 percent of HR Transformation programmes produce the desired results.[40] In other words, everybody's doing it, but nobody's doing it right.

Why don't these HR systems give us what we need?

Is there a way to 'do it right' when it comes to global HR transformation systems? All my experience to date suggests not, and here's why.

---

[40] https://www.ti-people.com/reversing-the-transformation-death-spiral

They erase the human factor

Recently I received a call from a talented HR Manager in a global pharmaceutical company. Her department was in the process of embarking on a massive HR transformation programme of exactly the kind I've described: new systems, centralised processes, managers owning and leading it, employees serving themselves, and universally applied processes at the core. The problem was, she'd decided to leave because of it — her Business Partner role just wasn't any fun now she couldn't respond to her customers' specific needs. This points to the heart of what's wrong with these systems: they sweep aside the human dimension. If, as a front-line HR person, you've traditionally been able to put in place innovative and responsive measures to meet your customer requirements, this ends once the launch button on these systems is pressed.

The starting point for these programmes is that human beings are assets that have to be managed. This industrial concept is quite compelling in that it implies when we centralise and simplify transactional tasks and automate them to maximise economies of scale, we've made a sensible decision. However, it's usually driven by the desire to save money, not to improve the employee experience.

They're based on standardised processes

When we in HR implement these systems, we fall into the same old trap: instead of asking whether a process is necessary we find a way of improving it instead, this time by moving it online so it's more readily accessible.

Not only that, but we irritate managers around the business. We say, 'Here you are, managers. We know you don't see the value in this process, and now it's your responsibility instead of ours.' A task they saw as a pain when it was carried out for them by HR becomes intolerable when they have to do it for themselves. And that's on top of the loss of the local HR person whom they knew, liked, and trusted. It's like the early days of unreliable supermarket self-checkouts, when we were left with the feeling that if we were forced to do the swiping and bagging ourselves we should at least be given a uniform, a badge, and a staff discount.

What's more, there's a lack of flexibility built in. By stripping out local inconsistencies in the name of efficiency, we force managers to use one clunky system. All the local interpretation and responsiveness has gone, and if you try to bring it back it increases costs. The upshot is, these systems aren't based on the needs of the end user, but on the desire of HR to be more process driven.

They take too long

Think about how many apps you've downloaded onto your smartphone in the last two to three years, which is about the length of time it takes to implement these enterprise-wide systems. There's now a proliferation of funky, amazing ones HR could implement quickly and cheaply, but when a business is 18 months into an HR Transformation programme all resources (including human) are diverted into that instead. 'Why', asks Finance incredulously, 'should you be allowed to spend money on some whizzy new gadget when you'll have a spanking new system in two years' time? And don't expect to integrate any of the latest HR thinking or technology into it once it's live — the money's gone.' When I was at the BBC my Head of Recruitment discovered a brilliant, low-cost recruitment technology that extracted the data from people's LinkedIn profiles, rather than them having to upload a CV or complete an application form. It saved huge amounts of time, but we struggled to push it through because of the new HR platform that was about to come online in two years. While we were spending a fortune on a cumbersome system, the world was moving on.

They're based on an outdated employment model

Another reason these systems don't work is that, despite the assumption they'll give us more robust data on our employees, they don't, because we increasingly 'employ' people who aren't in our organisations long term. As executive search and management consultancy Kennedy-Fitch says, 'Staff on demand is possibly one of the most impactful changes in managing organisations... Already now we witness an explosive growth of the "off payroll employee..." this growth will continue and in less than a decade, we can expect to have more than 50 percent no longer on our payroll and in 20 years from now (and possibly earlier), this may go to more than 80 percent.'[41]

Linked to this is the other misunderstanding baked into the system, which is the misguided notion that work is done in the teams enshrined in our organisational charts. If you've ever set up a global HR system I'm sure one of the first things you did was to work out who was in what team and at what level, because that would give individuals relevant permissions to increase salaries, carry out performance reviews, and view specific data. But as we know, although team members still report to managers the real work nowadays isn't done in set teams but in agile, dynamic groups. Take a look at talent and performance expert Marcus Buckingham's video about this, in which he criticises the 'parallel universe' HR lives in when it instigates systems that don't reflect the reality

---

[41] http://www.kennedyfitch.com/if-hr-transformation-is-dead-what-is-the-future-of-human-resources/

of modern organisations.[42] How does that help HR to improve our performance and talent management, let alone our credibility?

They typically don't work on mobile

These technologies work on PCs and laptops, but not always mobile, which is ridiculous given our new reliance on mobile technology. I recently gave a keynote speech for a global insurance company, in which the Chief Executive addressed his top HR people around the world. He said, 'The only time I have to use my PC now is to carry out the performance review process. For everything else I use my tablet or smartphone. How can this be right?' This has a serious impact on our credibility in HR.

To summarise, these systems cost a load of money, are a huge distraction when you're implementing them, won't deliver what you want, are based on a dying organisational and employment model, will prevent you from taking advantage of new technologies, will make your HR team miserable, and your customers unhappy. Apart from that, they're great! And yet so many companies think they're the answer to making HR more effective.

The reason I've spent so long discrediting these systems is I want to make ultra-sure your vision of HR transformation isn't running along these lines. If what you have in mind is a new system of this nature, just don't do it. There are better ways, which is what we'll come onto next.

---

[42] https://www.marcusbuckingham.com/rwtb/lets-get-real/

Quick recap

- Enterprise-wide HR Transformation systems are often mistakenly assumed to be the answer to HR change.
- They don't work, because
  - they don't take account of human needs;
  - they place too much emphasis on standardised processes;
  - they prevent you from taking advantage of new technologies;
  - they don't reflect the way work is done in organisations; and
  - they're not mobile friendly.
- There are better ways to implement change.

Segment and Target Your Employees

It's a sunny Saturday, and as you wander along your local high street you notice a new clothes shop has just opened. It seems inviting, so you pay it a visit. A pair of trousers catches your eye so you search for your size, only to notice something strange. The rack is filled with trousers, but they're all the same size and that seems to go for the other clothes in the shop too. It would be fine if the size were yours, but it's not. How bizarre and ridiculous. You leave in disappointment and vow never to darken the shop's doors again.

This is similar to the experience our employees have of HR. We expect them to conform to a uniform set of processes and systems, rather than treating them as individuals. Of course we can't design systems for each individual personally, but we can start to break down a homogeneous mass of people into more meaningful segments, the better to cater for their needs; this goes back to treating employees as consumers, which I touched on in Section 1. In this chapter I'll give you some examples of how you can treat your people in ways that mean something to them personally. It's all part of considering *who* you're creating your change for, which is essential to figure out before you carry out the transformation itself.

Before we go further, I'd like to address one of the worries HR often has when it contemplates treating people differently according to their needs, which is that segmentation might be discriminatory. Clearly there's a balance to be struck between the benefits of creating greater impact, relevance, and customer satisfaction, and the potential to be seen as unfair, and only you can decide where on that continuum you place yourself. But I continue to assert that a one-size-fits-all approach is based on cost-effectiveness of implementation and ease of monitoring, not on fairness. Let's go back to our clothes shop again. For the customers who happen to fit the size it sells, the clothes are ideal, but for the majority who don't they're annoying, irrelevant, and pointless. There's no doubt the shop is consistent, but is it fair for everyone?

Your key questions about your change should therefore be:

- will people love it?
- will it add value? and
- is it relevant to people's needs?

Let's learn from Marketing

No matter what kind of business you work in — business to business or business to consumer — your marketing department will be proficient at segmenting your customer base. They'll offer each group its own prices, product and service offerings, and routes to market, so the customers in them will buy more readily as a result. HR can learn from this, and there are three steps we can take to cater for the differing needs of various employee groups.

1. *Analyse and segment your end users*

   When you take the trouble to analyse your employees, you'll quickly realise they warrant a variety of offerings. The only area of HR in which I see this happening in a meaningful way is recruitment. Because recruiters have skills and mindsets more in common with marketers than with other more internally focused HR people, they woke up long ago to the notion that recruiting millennial coders requires a different approach to that of attracting senior executives. However, once their work is done, the new starter they've wooed so successfully is forced to slot into a system that ignores their individual preferences and treats them the same as everyone else. Welcome aboard!

A great example of how to segment and target people internally is Starbucks. Its HR analytics team decided to take a marketing approach to talent management and career development, by researching its employees. It uncovered three clusters: 'careerists' (highly ambitious and motivated by long-term career advancement), 'artists' (community-oriented and motivated by working for a local, socially responsible employer), and 'skiers' (money-focused and motivated by earning enough for their next passion project or skiing holiday). Once the team had these segments defined, it helped managers to tailor programmes to meet their varying needs in career development and training.

2. *Provide choices*

Once you know your employee groups, you can provide them with choices tailored to their individual characteristics. The area in which companies are already doing this best is usually that of reward, with HR offering a number of options to employees for them to pick what they prefer; examples are the option either to top up a pension or have a pay rise instead. It's a helpful way of avoiding accusations of discrimination, because staff themselves are in control of the process. However, despite its prevalence in reward, we in HR don't tend to offer line managers divergent ways of working with people in order to suit their personal preferences.

And yet this personalisation is perfectly possible. I was struck by the example of an HR Manager in one of our workshops, who told me she'd given line managers in her company the objective of gaining regular feedback from their staff, but that how they did it was up to them. To help, she presented them with some options: sending a poll survey text to a sample of their team members once a week, providing them with a couple of feedback apps they could use, or having one-off sessions in which they just listened to the individual people. What a great idea. Could you say to your line managers: 'What I want is for your new starters, after their first week of work, to feel engaged, connected, and confident they know the basics. Here's a range of mechanisms you could use.'

When you own the outcome, rather than the process, you automatically gear your activities towards what will work for particular interests rather than treating everyone the same.

3. *Personalise*

In our life outside work we expect and enjoy a level of personalisation in the services and products we use. We edit our phone apps to give us the notifications we want; we create our own playlists on Spotify; and we pre-set our car seats to our preferred driving position. We like the sensation of being in control that customisation gives us.[43] Think about when you receive personal recommendations from an online retailer; 35 percent of Amazon purchases and 75 percent of Netflix views come from what the companies suggest.

What could a consumer approach look like in your organisation? Here are two examples of how companies are trying to create not just 'an' employee experience, but 'my' employee experience. Wipro is a business outsourcing organisation based in India. Its HR people use the induction process to find out what's special and different about each new employee, including how they prefer to learn and be managed. This enables them to help managers adapt their style to make it more suitable, leading to a 33 percent increase in staff retention in the first six months of adopting this approach. PR agency Dynamo includes in its contracts what it's come to call the 'Don Draper clause', inspired by the TV series *Mad Men*. It introduced it in 2014, after a recruit insisted she would only take the job if Dynamo would guarantee to send her regular chocolate deliveries. The board thought, 'Why not?' and decided to extend it to all staff, with the result their contracts now include individualised treats like spa days, roller coaster rides, and Givenchy cosmetics. The key element of this is that it's based on what the particular employee wants, and the Dynamo Twitter

---

[43] https://www.psychologytoday.com/blog/cui-bono/201104/freedom-and-control

account captures people's excitement when they receive their gifts.[44]

You might be thinking this all sounds like a lot of effort, but bear this in mind: when you're not wasting time trying to get people to comply with a centralised system that doesn't work, you're freed up to create new options that will be more relevant and have impact. In planning your change there's no need to start from the assumption the outcome has to be the same for everybody. In fact, in shouldn't be. This is a new conceptual and philosophical notion to get your head around, but it's fundamental to creating change which is appreciated and credible. In the next chapter you'll learn how to characterise your employee groups.

---

[44] https://www.theguardian.com/small-business-network/2015/apr/02/staff-treats-unlimited-holiday-dynamo-pr

Action point

- In your workbook, identify three ways you could find out more about your employee base. This could include talking to your marketing department about research methods, doing a pulse survey, or interrogating the data you already have in a different way than usual. You can download your workbook here: https://disruptivehr.com/thehrchangetoolkitworkbook

Quick recap

- Successful businesses segment and target their customer bases because they know they'll sell more as a result.

- In the same way, HR gets better results if it treats employee groups according to their wants and needs.

- Offer your employees choices and the chance to choose and personalise their HR services.

- Your plans for change should be based on achieving outcomes that divergent groups appreciate and use, rather than on a one-size-fits-all system that's simple for HR to control and operate.

Create Employee Personas

The next step in understanding who you're designing your change for is to take a deep dive into who your employees are and how you can group them. As we saw in the last chapter, this will move you from a one-size-fits-all approach towards creating an environment which helps people to do their best work.

To start with let's think about how HR process design traditionally works. We identify the problem, consult key stakeholders, and then develop a process to meet the needs of the organisation. Note that I said the organisation, not the users, which is why we end up with systems that are wonderfully scalable, easy to monitor, consistently applied, and cost effective to implement. So far so good, but do they meet the needs of the people who will be using them?

I'm sure you take counsel from representatives of your users when you create something new, but picking one manager, one leader, and a couple of employees is hardly typical of the richness and diversity of your people. These example employees bring their personal agendas into the mix, and have probably been chosen by you on the basis of their role or level in the hierarchy rather than because they represent any particular motivation or interest. When you limit yourself to these functional divisions, you're falling into that perennial and most ironic of HR traps: ignoring the human factor.

The answer to this is 'user-centred design', which entails crafting a solution based on the needs and desires of the people who will be using it. And to know your users, you have to be able to describe them.

How to craft your personas

How can you go about grouping your people in a more meaningful way? We looked at creating personas for your Scary Six adversaries in the last section, so let's put your new skills to use in a more positive way for your employee base. The HR people I know who have used this technique have found it opened their eyes to their employees in ways they hadn't anticipated. There are two benefits of personas:

- they help you understand what different employee groups want and need, which in turn enables you to create suitable products and services for them, and

- they help you understand how to communicate with these groups, so you're able to sell in your changes successfully.

I'm not sure how much you know about developing consumer personas, but your Marketing colleagues have been doing it for years and it can work incredibly well for us in HR. It's based on the insight that a customer isn't an abstract concept but a living, breathing person who comes into your marketplace carrying their preconceived ideas, baggage, and emotions. In the same way as Marketing does for its customers, you can create fictionalised models to represent your target employee groups. In doing so you'll develop empathy for them, which means you'll be able to identify more readily with their needs and develop services they'll find useful and helpful.

What follows is a practical guide to creating your own personas. I suggest you gather your team together for this because not only will you need a diverse input from HR people with experience around the business, but you'll also find it a lot easier to gain buy-in from them if they've been involved. You have to *believe* in your personas — if you feel you're just doing it as a paper exercise it won't work. Give yourselves permission to have fun as well; take inspiration from a five-year-old child who's got an imaginary friend — to that child, their friend's persona is completely real! I suggest you create a maximum of four to six employee personas, because otherwise it can get confusing.

Start with the basics:

- Age
- Job function
- Years of experience
- Location
- Manager or not
- Personality type (if your company does personality assessments).

Then move onto the more interesting stuff. Here are some elements to consider:

- What are they called? Give each persona a name and picture.
- What's their personal background, such as where they worked before and why they're at your company now?
- What behavioural identifiers do they have, such as motives, attitudes, and trigger points?
- What do they want from their jobs?
- What do they love doing in their own time?
- What do they read?

- How do they consume media?

- What's their income and how much do they spend — have they got a big mortgage or expensive kids?

Go as deep as you can with this, and remember you're basing your findings on both your research data and your collective experience of your employee base; in fact, you'll find you need relatively few facts and figures at all. I'll give you an example from my days at the BBC. There we had a large number of people who'd worked in the organisation for many years, typically in a similar career path. They were in their late 40s, married with kids, placed a high value on education (and their pension), and were members of the union. What we would normally do is stop there. We've done the easy bit such as age and length of service, but in creating a persona you're going to breathe life into that person. Your representation of them should be so rich and detailed it feels as if they might leap from the page; if you and your team can see them, you can believe them. This means being specific so if you're imagining their favourite TV show, for instance, name the show instead of putting 'cop dramas'. It makes a difference. What do they read? What do they do at the weekend? Some of this you'll make up but you'll be doing it using your common sense. You could start with imagining their day from the moment they wake up; if they have kids, for instance, this will be a different experience to if they don't. Then go through their day hour by hour until they travel home and go about their evening activities. This helps you to see them as a whole person.

Virgin Trains, who you'll gather by now I'm a huge fan of in terms of its consumer-led approach to its employees, created personas by imagining a day in the life of its staff. As it happens it chose job roles rather than personas, because it was most interested in what it was like to be a person doing that job, such as a train chef or a customer services assistant. Researchers accompanied a selection of staff from the beginning of their day to the end, arriving at their house before they went to work, dropping their kids off at school with them, and experiencing what it was like to travel to their job (such as the nature of their journey and the parking experience once they arrived). In observing them throughout the day they noticed how they talked with other team members, when they interacted with their customers, and if they ever connected with their team leaders. They learned about the most stressful points in their day and saw when they had down time. They also witnessed their use of technology, such as their smartphones and their PCs, which helped Virgin to develop opportunities for bite-sized learning and communication. It was an extraordinarily smart exercise.

You may find your marketing department already has something like this in place for your external customers. I once helped a pension company in Melbourne, Australia, with its HR strategy. As I entered the reception I was blown away by a series of huge posters which were based on its customer personas. The depth of information it had on these people was staggering, including their favourite reading material and what they liked to cook. When I asked the company how impactful this had been in helping it shape and communicate its products and services, it said it had made a fundamental difference to how it built relationships with its customers. The one thing it wasn't doing, however, was using these techniques internally for its own employees. So you can see the untapped potential of these personas for HR.

One of the barriers you may face is people claiming they're not representative in a statistically valid way, and

I've certainly had this myself. I remember when I had feedback from an engineer in a manufacturing company who challenged me on this, and I replied, 'You're right, they won't be scientifically exact, but you're not basing them on nothing. For instance, if you've got a predominantly male workforce, don't create four female personas — make sure they're indicative of your employee base. And secondly, you're not trying to be statistically representative, you're trying to be human. You're using your existing data, your common sense, and your collective personal experience to create them. You'll be surprised at how, when you've done your four or five personas, they cover most of your people.' In some instances you're going to find it hard to come up with the ideal one, but this process isn't supposed to be perfect. All it's supposed to do is enable you to think about what matters to your people in their career development, and how they might want to work and be communicated with.[45]

How to use your personas

Once you've created your personas, you'll probably find that multiple uses for them will occur to you. You'll instantly see why some of your communications aren't working, or why certain incentive schemes aren't being taken up. In the same way you'll gain ideas about how you can design your services more effectively for each group. One use is in role playing, another technique which requires you to shrug off your inhibitions and embrace your playful side. Who said HR transformation had to be hard work? By pretending to be one of your personas you're

---

[45] You can see a couple of examples here: https://hrtrendinstitute. com/2017/05/11/personas

switching on your creative empathy; it's a powerful way of sensing what it's like to be someone else. Role playing isn't just an application of personas, by the way, it's also an incredibly useful tool for testing out all sorts of ideas in a safe way, and is increasingly used in the development of products and services.

My thinking in this area has been inspired by some consultancy work I did for HR people at a major optician chain. We worked together to plan how they would change their approach to performance management, talent, and induction, and they came up with some fascinating ideas based on role playing. At the beginning I assumed it would be a purely academic exercise but the results amazed me. I asked them to find a way to get under the skin of some of their employee groups by 'becoming' them — and they did. They stopped talking about 'they' and started saying 'we' and 'I'; they even adopted their language and mindset. It made me realise how little we do this in HR, or even in business as a whole. Imagine if you were to use this valuable technique to practice communicating changes in your pension scheme, for instance; you could gauge the reactions of certain types of employee, and by rehearsing the reactions you think they might have, design your communications accordingly.

Action point

- In your workbook, decide your next steps for creating your employee personas. These could including identifying what data to interrogate, which members of your team to brainstorm with, and what timetable is most suitable for you. At this stage, try not to jump the gun by making assumptions about what the personas will consist of; it's better to keep an open mind until you have the information in front of you. You can download your workbook here: https://disruptivehr.com/thehrchangetoolkitworkbook.

Quick recap

- Creating employee personas enables you to step into the shoes of people in your segments, so you can better evaluate HR services from their different perspectives.

- Create them by using your existing data, your experience, your common sense, and your imagination.

- Bring your personas to life by envisaging the details of their daily lives, and make sure you can believe in them.

- When you have them, allow yourself to be influenced by them when you create and communicate your services. Role playing is one way of doing this.

Beware of the 90/10 Rule

When you're considering who to design your change for, it's easy to make assumptions that have come from years of doing things a certain way. One of these is what I call the 90/10 rule. In HR we tend to design our processes around either the top or bottom 10 percent of employees. The top 10 percent — the super-talent in the top right-hand box of the nine-box grid — are showered with attention through fast-track programmes, promotions and higher bonuses. This is usually supported by boardroom politics. I've always found it interesting that, despite the CEOs I've worked for over the years asking me to make deep cuts into my HR budgets, they were always reluctant to axe one of the priciest items in the HR portfolio: the High Potentials Programme. After all, many of them had been part of this themselves and it didn't do them any harm, did it? At the other end of the scale, the bottom 10 percent of employees are the people we don't trust to do the right thing, and whom we target with the vast majority of our employment policies, processes, and performance management procedures. We create these with good intentions because we want to catch any problems before they occur, but this means we design them for the lowest common denominator.

There are serious downsides to this approach, the main one of which is staring us in the face: we're ignoring the vast majority of the organisation. We can't afford to do this any longer, and here's why.

The problem with the 90/10 rule for the top 10 percent

I've never felt entirely comfortable with High Potential Programmes, and recently I've come to the conclusion my instincts have been proven right. Recent research by management consultancy CEB[46] suggests that 73 percent of them fail to produce a positive business outcome. We shouldn't be surprised by this statistic, as there are glaring errors in how we execute them; the following three problems ought to be sufficient for us to pause and question.

We pump money and time into an elite group — one which is possibly not the brightest and best in any case

The data we use to identify high potentials is flawed by our outdated performance management processes, which have an inherent rater bias. One of my clients was disappointed when, at the launch of his new High Potentials Programme, his opinion was that 'out of 24 people, there were probably only seven who had any real potential'. This was despite HR spending several weeks nailing the right criteria and coaching senior leaders to help them make sound decisions. How many times have you looked at your Hi-Po nominations and thought, 'Really? Are they actually the best?' In my experience we recommend people for this status for a whole range of dubious and subjective reasons, the most common being that the manager is a perceived flight risk, as an alternative to a pay rise, and because of not knowing how to say no. When I was at Serco, for instance, we ran a leadership course in

---

[46] https://www.cebglobal.com/insights/high-potentials.html

which it regularly transpired that about half the delegates weren't as high performing as we'd assumed they were. They'd been sent on it because they had a great relationship with their boss or were doing a job that played to their strengths, but when they were later promoted into a management role they often didn't perform well.

High Potentials Programmes are inherently divisive

These programmes create a group of perceived favourites, who now have the additional burden of high expectation on their shoulders. What's more, these annointed ones can become frustrated by a lack of immediate promotional rewards now they've been earmarked as 'special'. This results in a group of pressured, insecure leaders and managers with an insatiable appetite for reward and success — a toxic combination.

The programmes lack transparency

Leaders worry about the neglected 90 percent discovering they're not in the elite group. According to CEB, this results in up to a third of businesses concealing from the high potentials that they've been identified as such, creating the crazy situation in which the organisations have a programme the members don't even know they're on.

Like many of our traditional HR talent tools, the High Potentials Programme belongs to a different age — when careers were more linear and predictable, when structures were less flat, when 'career paths' made sense, and when we thought of talent in terms of the people who work for us rather than thinking beyond our borders. The truth is the best people at the top will always be okay, ensuring their voices are heard and pushing for the best opportunities. We don't have to worry about them too much, and we certainly don't need to play the HR parent with them when it comes to designing change.

The problem with the 90/10 rule for the bottom 10 percent

On the other hand, there's a danger inherent in designing change around the weak minority. When we do this we inflict constraining policies and processes on people who are capable of more, and who have no intention of behaving in the same way as the bottom 10 percent in any case. It's tempting to tell ourselves if the policy doesn't apply to the 90 percent they can just ignore it, but there are three main reasons why this isn't good enough.

It discourages innovation and pro-activity

When we force people in the majority to carry out a procedure designed for the lowest common denominator, we patronise them and — even worse — sap their ability to think for themselves. How irritating is it to be treated as a poor performer when you know you're not? Does it make you feel like you want to do your best work? Do you feel confident taking a risk that might result in a mistake, when you know the outcome will be a tutting rewrite of the company's procedures manual? This is not a recipe for encouraging people to be brilliant.

It deters poor performers from improving

A brilliant article in the *Harvard Business Review*[47] refers to this as the Pygmalion Effect. In George Bernard Shaw's play, Eliza Doolittle famously says: 'You see, really

---

[47] https://hbr.org/2003/01/pygmalion-in-management

and truly, apart from the things anyone can pick up (the dressing and the proper way of speaking, and so on), the difference between a lady and a flower girl is not how she behaves but how she's treated. I shall always be a flower girl to Professor Higgins because he always treats me as a flower girl and always will; but I know I can be a lady to you because you always treat me as a lady and always will.' If we design services around people with the assumption they can't do something, the chances are they won't; in other words, if we assume they're useless managers that's how they'll behave. On the other hand if our starting point is that they're capable of managing well rather than us constantly compensating for poor behaviour, we'll most likely see an improvement.

It rewards poor behaviour

When we spend lots of time on our 'problem children', we lavish them with our undivided support and attention. Where's the incentive for them to change?

So don't worry about the outliers. The best will be fine with or without your help, and if you gear your actions towards the worst you'll only stifle the rest. That doesn't mean you shouldn't have any policies or procedures aimed at these groups, only that they're best left as back seat passengers rather than being in the driving seat of your HR transformation. It's the 80 percent in the middle who should be the main focus of your attention; your job is to cater for everybody, not to nanny and control the minority.

Now you've explored who to create your change for, in the next chapter you'll learn the techniques to use when you put your transformation into action.

Action point

- In your workbook, list the policies and procedures you consider to be aimed purely at your top
and bottom 10 percent of performers. If you were
to ignore these two groups, what would be left?
You can download your workbook here: https://
disruptivehr.com/thehrchangetoolkitworkbook.

Quick recap

- When you gear your change towards the top or
bottom 10 percent of performers, you ignore the
vast majority of your organisation.

- The high potential group isn't necessarily valid
and is perfectly capable of looking after itself in
any case.

- The 'trouble maker' group shouldn't drive your
change either, because they'll skew what you do
in a way that both demotivates everyone else and
discourages them from improving.

- Gear your HR transformation towards the 80 percent instead.

Think Products, Not Services

HR is all about creating and managing services, right? Well, yes, but that's not the most helpful way of seeing it when you want to transform it. Here's where I'd like you to start thinking about your services as products instead, and there are a number of reasons for this. The first is when we in HR develop a service, we tend to assume it's underpinned by a process — in our case a streamlined, efficient one. This encourages us to have a process-based mindset, which is necessarily focused on the needs of the organisation rather than those of our diverse end users. In other words, we lose sight of our customers as living, breathing people and start seeing them as units or assets. You can see this in the language we use when we talk about service creation; we say we're 'rolling out' a service, for instance, a term which embodies a blanket process. When we think of a product, we're more inclined to focus on whether (and how) it's being used. Do the various elements of it work well together? Does it achieve what it's supposed to? Are people clear about why they should use it? This is what's now being called 'user-centred design'. As soon as we make the mental switch from service to product design, we automatically have more of a marketing head on. We think about outcomes rather than inputs, and about selling the change rather than expecting people to buy into it.

Interestingly, Deloitte now recognises that a product development mentality is increasingly important in HR, but that only 10 percent of companies rate themselves as being excellent at user-designed thinking.[48] It has also discovered some other interesting trends. As a business, it carries out what is in my view one of the few all-encompassing annual HR surveys that's truly progressive. In their 2017 report,[49] they review a couple of important ways in which companies are looking at user-designed thinking in a product design context. They refer to Cisco, IBM, GE, and Airbnb, all of whom are using their employees to collect ideas about workplace design, benefits, and rewards, and to design new approaches on the back of that. They also mention companies such as Nike, the Commonwealth Bank of Australia, and Deutsche Telekom, and how they're making use of user-designed thinking to improve their employee experiences. These companies have redesigned their induction, recruitment, and employee self-service applications, while most of us are still stuck in traditional service development thinking.

In the following two chapters of 'Design Your Change', you'll learn about product road maps, branding your services, creating a minimum viable product so you don't have to be perfect before you launch, and developing products that are right for now rather than being right forever (because what is?). This will give you the opportunity to think about new product development techniques such as agile product development, creating a minimum viable product, and user-designed thinking. By the end of it, you'll be well on your way to being a cutting-edge product and service designer.

---

[48] https://www2.deloitte.com/insights/us/en/focus/human-capital-trends/2017/improving-the-employee-experience-culture-engagement.html

[49] https://www2.deloitte.com/insights/us/en/focus/human-capital-trends/2017/improving-the-employee-experience-culture-engagement.html

Action point

- In your workbook, pick two or three of your key services. How would you re-imagine them if you were to look at them as products instead? You can download your workbook here: https://disruptivehr.com/thehrchangetoolkitworkbook.

Quick recap

- When you think of your services as products, you're more likely to have a user-centred design mentality.

- You'll also free yourself from blanket processes that don't deliver the results your users want.

How Product Designers Do it

We've already made the point that seeing your services as products is the best approach, but how does product design work? This chapter unpicks the process and explains how you can launch a new product (or service) far more quickly and easily than the way you're doing now. To make it simple, I'm focusing on the product design processes favoured by two companies that have a forward-thinking approach to the subject: global design agency IDEO and Apple. In doing so I'll uncover the secrets of the world's best product creators, and how they develop products their customers love and recommend. If you'd like your employees to feel the same way about your HR services as they do about their iPhones, this is for you.

Let's start with IDEO, a company at the forefront of understanding the needs of the user and designing its products around them. For IDEO, the end result is based on a genuine understanding of how the products will be used, and its process for this, which it calls Human-Centered Design,[50] involves both observing the end user and putting itself in their shoes. Here's how it does it.

---

[50] https://www.usertesting.com/blog/2015/07/09/how-ideo-uses-customer-insights-to-design-innovative-products-users-love

What we can learn from IDEO

1. *Observation and experiencing the user's activity*

   In this phase, IDEO observes the end user so it can learn from them. As part of this, it identifies behaviour patterns, pain points, and moments when users find it difficult to do something — these are opportunities for improvement. Think of the example I gave of Virgin Trains following its people around to observe their day — this is a classic observation technique.

   Although I didn't call it anything fancy at the time, this is what I also did in a small way at the BBC. When I first arrived, I was horrified to discover how many of my team members who were responsible for designing policies and procedures hadn't witnessed a television programme being planned or filmed: they'd never seen the news go out, they'd never been part of the filming, and they'd never sat in any pre-production meetings. I could see we needed to put this right, and as a result we learned that some of the processes we'd set up were completely impractical for their end users to comply with, which led to us redesigning them. So make sure you're close to what it's like to use your own systems. Do you know how an operative in one of your factories spends their day, for instance? If you don't, how on earth can you possibly design products (or services) for them to use? When you forge ahead with improvements without having deeply understood the needs of your user base and employee personas, you'll come up with a poorer set of answers.

2. *Ideation*

This is a brainstorming phase, and one which — importantly — stays focused on the needs and desires of the people IDEO is designing for. What's your normal starting point for developing something new? If it's to create a series of small, incremental changes or improvements to an existing process, you'll be constrained in your thinking. But if you give yourself permission to think big, or even off the wall, you're more likely to come up with an idea that will wow people. For instance, if you want to encourage your customer service assistants, your television producers, or your train drivers to have regular conversations with their people, brainstorming a big question will generate more ideas than asking, 'How can we improve our performance management process?' Instead of thinking about how you could improve what you already do, you could use techniques like the Three Whys to get to the heart of what you want to achieve.

If you were a fly on the wall of a creative marketing agency, you'd witness the ideation process on an almost daily basis. At a brainstorming session the walls are filled with countless ideas, some of which are completely stupid but a handful of which could be brilliant. We in HR don't engage in this kind of creativity often enough, even though we're capable of it, because we have a service mentality.

3. *Rapid prototyping*

In HR we tend to fix on an idea, disappear for weeks or even months to develop it to perfection, and then launch it with a fanfare — only to wonder why most people don't like it. This desire to come up with the ideal solution comes from a good place: we want to be accurate and understand the impact it will have on our organisation. But it doesn't lend itself to creating services people want and need. Instead, IDEO builds a rapid prototype of an idea so as to make it tangible and testable. It doesn't have to look beautiful, it just has to do a good enough job to be worth trying out.

4. *User feedback*

This is the most critical phase of a human-centred design process, because without knowing what your end users think, you won't know if what you've created suits their needs. Nor will you know how to evolve it. In HR we're not bad at consulting people, but we tend to do it only at the beginning and end of a new service development. What we don't do is collect regular user feedback, which is what IDEO does.

5. *Iteration*

As IDEO says, once you have feedback you can use it to inform the changes you need to make to improve it. It's important to keep testing and tweaking until you've fine-tuned your service. This takes patience and commitment, but with each iteration you'll learn more about how to create a service that delights your users.

6. *Implementation*

Now is the moment you've been waiting for, which is when your new service goes out into the world to be used by everyone it's intended for.

Remember every time you update it, you can go back to the first step — that way you make sure your services continue to reflect the needs and wants of your end users.

I find this six-step process to be incredibly useful. In my experience, if we rush to finish something it can be hard to improve it after it's launched because everyone's bought into (or rejected) it by then. This lack of testing and prototyping has a serious impact on our credibility, because not only do we tend to produce services that don't hit the mark, but people wonder what the heck we do all day when we know we work unbelievably hard. We're just not making the stages of our work visible, that's all.

What we can learn from Apple

Apple[51] is the second of my ideal product design companies, and, with its intuitive and sleek products that routinely delight its customers, is known as one of the best designers in the world. There are three basic principles it employs, which we in HR can learn from and adopt in our service development.

The first is that it regularly reviews its products in development, which maintains the pace and focus on its pipeline; there's a meeting for this every Monday. I remember working with a fantastic guy at the BBC called Erik Huggers who'd previously worked for Microsoft, and who used to get frustrated with what he saw as our 'television mindset'. If we were commissioning a new series

---

[51] https://thenextweb.com/apple/2012/01/24/this-is-how-apples-top-secret-product-development-process-works/

such as *Peaky Blinders*, we'd take a couple of years to move it from concept to screens; the speed of the launch was determined purely by how long it took to become perfect. Obviously for programmes such as the weekly soaps we had a more time-pressured approach, but for large-scale commissions this was a typical attitude. Erik used to talk about shipping products rather than launching services, and I think this language is useful for us in HR: how do we keep a relentless focus on a development until it's in a good enough state to 'ship'? When I look back on my own failures in launching new services, I now realise it was because the manager developing it would go away to work on it and then re-emerge several months later with something that wasn't necessarily fit for purpose. I should have said, 'This is important, so we're going to focus on it weekly until we can test it and get it out there.' We didn't have a fast enough pace.

The other way Apple succeeds in creating such beautiful products is in its insistence on simplicity. As Steve Jobs used to say, 'Quality is more important than quantity.' Can you imagine if we had weekly new product meetings in HR like they do at Apple? We'd never get through all our improvements and changes because there are so many of them. Once the Divisional HR Heads have prioritised their needs and the Centres of Expertise Managers have initiated projects in their areas, we have a smorgasbord of activity based on what a range of people believe to be high priority, rather than on what the most important end users want and need. This scattergun approach also leads us to chuck a load of confusing changes at people, sometimes without realising that Finance, for instance, is doing something similar that we could tap into. If we were to prioritise two or three important new services — ones that would improve our credibility, our responsiveness, and our speed of implementation — it would be transformational for HR. This means saying 'no' to some initiatives.

The final practice at Apple I'd like to highlight is something it calls the 'EPM Mafia'. This is made up of the Engineering Program Manager and the Global Supply Manager for a particular product, and their job is to move it from design to production. Again, see the focus. Do we in HR have one senior person whose responsibility it is to get that service out there? If we've only got two or three projects on the go at once we can afford to have a high-ranking leader, whose credibility rests on getting results, championing each one.

Launching quickly and easily with Minimum Viable Products

Central to the modern product design industry is the concept of the Minimum Viable Product (MVP). If you've ever read *The Lean Startup* [52] by Eric Ries you'll be familiar with this; what it means is the version of a product which allows the creator to collect the maximum amount of validated learning about its users with the least effort. There are several benefits to this approach. You can:

- test your understanding of whether your service is needed before it goes wide;

- accelerate your team's learning about what your users want;

- adapt to your customers' needs during the iteration phase;

---

[52] *The Lean Startup: How Constant Innovation Creates Radically Successful Businesses,* by Eric Ries. Portfolio Penguin, 2011.

- minimise wasted time by focusing on the minimum number of features needed for launch; and

- get to market more quickly.[53]

Embedded within this is the notion that progress is better than perfection, and we in HR get nervous about that. We don't like the idea of running into compliance or legal complications, or of upsetting unions, and so we avoid putting a new offering out there that isn't completely accurate and that we can't see working as a universally applied, end-to-end process. But this isn't always the best way of delivering services people will be delighted to use.

How 'minimal' should your MVP be? In the words of Eric Ries, 'Probably much more minimum than you think.' So instead of launching an upgrade model to your reward system, you invite people to sign up to be notified when it's upgraded. That way you're testing how many people are interested in your plans and finding out what they might want. You can also use simple channels to launch your idea, so instead of laying on an expensive training programme on how managers can have regular conversations with their staff, you could record a podcast or a short video showing what one looks like and get feedback on that. Or instead of investing in a whole new learning management system you could take a key topic such as how to negotiate, and use Facebook Workplace or your own intranet to share a couple of short videos from your Finance Director on how to do it. I like this light touch approach, because it means you start moving more quickly and are able to trial your ideas with early adopters, building from that point.

---

[53] https://www.interaction-design.org/literature/article/minimum-viable-product-mvp-and-design-balancing-risk-to-gain-reward

Can you see how thinking 'product, not service' will get you to where you want to be more quickly and easily than the traditional approach? And can you envisage how this will help your services become more appreciated, credible, and user friendly as a result? Learning from, and adopting, product design techniques might feel philosophically difficult, but once you get your head around it you'll find yourself launching relevant and appreciated new services with far fewer resources than you currently rely on. As a bonus, it takes some of the pressure off you to be perfect every time because you're not aiming to be. With the amount of complaining about HR that goes on in most organisations it can be easy to feel sensitive to criticism, especially when you work so hard every day to service people's needs. But now you've got a way to give them what they want in ways that are both useful to them and easier for you. There aren't many win–wins in business, so let's take the ones on offer.

Action point

- In your workbook, list the current service improvement projects you currently have. Pick the three that are most important for HR in terms of both credibility for you and benefit for users, and park the rest. You can download your workbook here: https://disruptivehr.com/thehrchangetoolkitworkbook.

Quick recap

- Product designers are experts in user-centred design and start their design process from a deep understanding of their users. So should you.

- Feeling free to brainstorm, and then to rapidly test and iterate your design, will enable you to create services your users will enjoy and appreciate.

- If you scale back the number of new service developments you have, you'll be able to drive through the key ones and make a bigger impact.

- When you test and improve a minimum viable product, rather than a full-scale 'perfected' solution, you can launch new services quickly and easily.

Design Experiences, Not Processes

Type 'employee experience' into LinkedIn and you'll see what a buzz there is around the concept right now; the last time I tried it came up with over four million results. This is supported by the Deloitte survey[54] I mentioned earlier, in which creating a favourable employee experience is presented as a major trend; it seems we're all wanting to find ways to create the right conditions for our employees to thrive and do their best work. However, that same survey also reveals only 22 percent of companies consider themselves to be excellent at building a differentiated experience for their staff — one which also aligns with their employer and consumer brands. Why are we finding it so difficult to reach this holy grail? It's partly because of our obsession in HR with processes, which gets in the way of us considering the overall experience. This process focus is supported by the siloed nature of our teams (reward teams, performance teams, training teams, and so on), who rarely get the opportunity to think beyond the area for which they're responsible. If they could take a holistic view they'd find it easier to see things from the perspective of the employee having an experience, rather than from that of the processes themselves.

---

[54] https://www2.deloitte.com/uk/en/pages/human-capital/articles/introduction-human-capital-trends.html

I discovered that one online retailer has a forward-thinking approach to this, so I talked to their HR Director about it. The company used to produce paper-based catalogues, so you can imagine the huge changes it's been through in its move to a digital format. The entire business now works in new ways which are all based around the customer experience, and its HR department wanted to reflect that within its own team.

The starting point was to identify the experiences it wanted its colleagues (as it calls them) to have, in relation to the company's consumer brand. The HR team asked: 'Which part of the colleague experience matters most in relation to the customer experience?' This led them to focus on creating the right conditions to energise colleagues; rather than simply acknowledging the importance of recognition, for instance, they now also encompass IT and physical working spaces.

In order to create these experiences, they realised they needed more insights into how people around the business felt and who they were, which led to them develop a series of personas. They also stopped doing a lot of work that wasn't adding value such as engagement surveys, annual performance gradings, and many of their communications; this freed up at least two days a week for HR to organise and participate in cross-functional and cross-business 'squads' to work on colleague experiences. Now the HR leadership team only plans ahead in three month 'sprints', with no cumbersome plans. It saves time to focus on what matters, has energised its HR team, and it goes without saying that it's also massively improved HR's relationship with the rest of the business. There have been other benefits as well. HR teams now work collaboratively, are freer in their thinking, have a joined-up approach to their work, and have reduced their defensiveness about their existing processes. Now, instead of improving an existing procedure they look afresh at what's needed and what will help employees the most.

What are the employee experiences you want to create? One might be, 'We want people to feel free to do their best work.' If you were to aim for this you can imagine how many different processes would feed into it, such as performance management and reward. For instance, if your people are bonused on achieving personal targets, but someone spots a gap in the market the business isn't currently exploiting, would the reward process you've created support them in filling that gap? Or would they decide it wasn't worth risking their bonus in order to make the company more money? You can see how thinking from the standpoint of an experience takes you in all sorts of directions that would never occur to you if your starting point was a process.

Action point

- In your workbook, describe the main experiences you would like your employees to have, related to both your internal and external brand, and to your employee personas. Then list the processes that either help or hinder that experience. You'll find this hard to do on your own, so see it as a starting point to discuss with your team. You can download your workbook here: https://disruptivehr.com/thehrchangetoolkitworkbook.

Quick recap

- Creating an employee experience that both fosters good work and aligns with a company's consumer brand is something many organisations want to achieve but find difficult.

- This is both because HR tends to start from processes rather than experiences, and because of the siloed nature of HR teams.

- Shop Direct is an excellent example of an HR department that has created ways for its people to work collaboratively so it reflects the needs of the business.

Section 6

Help Your Change to Happen

Hopefully it's clear by now traditional approaches to change don't work. When we create top-down transformation programmes based on command and control methodologies, we assume change is a linear process that can be plotted onto a Gantt chart. We think if we draft a strong enough business case, provide the logic, and then apply the levers of coercion and reward that transformation will magically happen as a result. This is a mistake we in HR have been making for too long. Because change can't happen without *people*, who think, feel, and behave in certain ways because of their intrinsic nature. Much as we might sometimes love to we can't change human psychology, so we're best to go with the grain of how irrational we are rather than to force change upon subjects who don't want to comply. That's why I've called this section 'Help Your Change to Happen' rather than 'Implement Change', because change isn't something you can do *to* people, it's something you can only help them to welcome.

So far, in exploring your preparation for change I've focused mainly on the importance of HR having an adult-to-adult and consumer-based approach to employees. Now I'm moving into the realm of implementing change, and here's where the human element comes to the fore. I'll be honest: in the past, my least successful attempts at leading change have always been when I neglected to base my desired transformation on how human beings think, feel, behave, communicate, and are intrinsically motivated. This is why this section will show you:

- why your employees think and behave the way they do;
- what that means for how you try to change leaders' and managers' approaches to working;

- how you can encourage your front-line staff to change;
- the best ways of testing and launching your change;
- what technologies can help with this;
- how to judge whether what you've done has worked; and
- what do to if it doesn't pan out the way you expect.

In doing so, you'll learn how to create the change you want in a more effective and less stressful way than you've experienced before.

Understand Why Humans Behave the Way They Do

If you want to make life hard for yourself when you're trying to change things, it's pretty simple: assume people will follow your instructions, and as long as they understand the reasoning and are incentivised appropriately, they'll go along with it. This, as you've probably discovered, never works. Instead, months of frustration ensue as you wonder why nobody actions your sensible ideas, even when they've sat opposite you in meetings and agreed with them. On the other hand, if you want to make change easier both for you and for everyone else, you need to understand some of the basic principles of human psychology. So let's go on what I hope will be a fascinating journey into our minds in order to learn how to use human behaviour as a lever for change, rather than forcing rigid HR processes onto people. Then in the following chapter I'll explain what you can do to lead change while taking this knowledge into account.

Naturally we each of us have our individual backgrounds, upbringings, fears, and preferences, and these shape our behaviour, but there are a number of patterns that are typical of all humans. I'm no psychology expert, but because I'm so fascinated by this area I've read stacks of books about it and have identified five key themes you need to embrace if you're to change both HR and others around your organisation. They are that:

- we're programmed to think emotionally rather than rationally;

- we want to be like everyone else;

- we're lazy and will do what's easiest;

- we do what we've always done; and

- we're more frightened of loss than excited by gain.

Let's look at each of these five human traits as they relate to change.

We're programmed to think in certain ways

No matter now individual we may assume we are (and of course, we do have our personal characteristics), we humans can't help thinking broadly the same way whether we like it or not. There are three or four excellent writers who have come to similar conclusions about this, and the first I'll talk about is Daniel Kahneman. In his book *Thinking, Fast and Slow*,[55] he explains why we choose one set of behaviours over another because of what he calls System One and System Two thinking. System One is automatic — it's our animal self, coming to the fore. When we use this our behaviour is involuntary and emotional, leading us to take short cuts, follow habitual patterns, make intuitive judgements, rely on unconscious biases and stereotypes, and jump to conclusions. System Two is rational — it's our more human and controlled self. When we use this system our behaviour is deliberate, analytical and logical, leading us to take our time over decisions and make more effort with our thinking. The crucial point

---

[55] *Thinking, Fast and Slow*, by Daniel Kahneman. Penguin, 2012.

Kahneman makes is that when the chips are down, System One will almost always win over System Two.

Other writers, including Chip and Dan Heath (*Switch*[56]), Steve Peters (*The Chimp Paradox*[57]), and David Rock (*Your Brain at Work*[58]), use different analogies to Kahneman, but they still describe our behaviour as the result of a battle our brains are constantly engaged in between our irrational, responsive, automatic side and our logical, deliberate, analytical side. What's more, like Kahneman, they all conclude that whenever that battle arises the former will win out.

And yet our traditional approach to change is to appeal to people's intellectual abilities, not to their emotions; every time we do that in HR we set up a conflict. In *Switch*, the Heath brothers talk about our System One type thinking as being the rider and System Two as being the elephant; when the rider tries to control his elephant he always loses because the animal is too big and strong for him unless he uses some clever tactics. Continuing this animal theme, Peters describes our brains as having both a chimp and a human in them. The chimp is the emotional, responsive element and the human is the more rational — and guess who wins? Again, the point is this: if you're trying to get managers to behave in new ways, you need to appeal to their System One thinking

[56] *Switch: How to Change Things When Change is Hard*, by Chip and Dan Heath. Random House Business, 2011.

[57] *The Chimp Paradox: The Acclaimed Mind Management Programme to Help You Achieve Success, Confidence and Happiness*, by Steve Peters. Vermilion, 2012.

[58] *Your Brain at Work: Strategies for Overcoming Distraction, Regaining Focus, and Working Smarter All Day Long*, by David Rock. HarperCollins, 2009.

(the elephant or the chimp) rather than relying on System Two (the rider or the human).

So your first challenge is to recognise that people are programmed to think and behave in these ways, and to find ways of working with them.

We want to be like everyone else

You'll have heard this element of human psychology called the herd mentality (those animals again), and to explain this more fully I'm going to relate just one example of many I could have chosen. One of the originators of this thinking is Solomon Asch, who conducted a fascinating experiment in the 1950s.[59] He showed participants a picture of a straight line on one side of a book; on the opposite page were three lines of differing length labelled A, B, and C. One of them, line C, was the same length as the original, and the research subjects were asked to choose which one it was. When they were asked in isolation over 99 percent gave the right answer (it wasn't a difficult test). But when Asch set up groups of participants who'd been primed to give the wrong answer first, and then asked new participants to choose the matching line, only 25 percent gave the right answer. When asked why, they admitted they hadn't believed their answer but had gone along with the group for fear of being ridiculed or considered peculiar.

Think about how marketers already make clever use of this insight into human nature. How often have you been sucked in by the 'popular' or 'trending now' options on Netflix, for instance? And how could you use it in HR? Because if everyone around you is working in old

---

[59] https://www.simplypsychology.org/asch-conformity.html

ways, why would it make sense to be the one to stand out and do things differently? Can you make it less intimidating *not* to be like everyone else?

We're lazy and will do what's easiest

You may have heard this trait described as 'following the path of least resistance' or 'picking the low hanging fruit'. What's fascinating about the psychological research[60] in this area is that whenever we have more than one option to choose from we'll almost always pick the easier one and *convince ourselves it's the better one as well.* We do this without realising it, because we feel more comfortable with our laziness if we think it's achieving a worthwhile result at the same time. In HR we tend to overcomplicate change and make it appear difficult, rather than recognising there's a default position within us to take the simple route. How can you make it seem easy for people to choose new ways of leading and managing?

We do what we've always done

Habit and productivity expert Charles Duhigg has researched the power of habits and how hard they are to break. I'm sure you can see this in your own behaviour — I know I do. I always dry my hair after I've brushed my teeth, for instance, for no other reason than it's what I'm used to. In fact, although we don't realise it, our habits were formed long ago because of the series of cues and rewards that came with them at the time; it's easier for us

---

[60] https://www.forbes.com/sites/carolinebeaton/2017/02/22/new-research-shows-that-were-wired-to-take-the-path-of-least-resistance/

to stay with an established pattern than to create a new groove. How can you create new cues and sufficient rewards to make it appear worthwhile for your managers to break their habits?

We're more frightened by loss than excited by gain

In his book *Nudge* [61] Richard Thaler says, 'Roughly speaking, losing something makes you twice as miserable as gaining the same thing makes you happy.' You might want to read that again so it sinks in. This aversion to loss is a well-known phenomenon in behavioural science and explains why, for instance, if you were to lose £10 you'd have to find £20 to get back to your previous emotional state. And yet most of our efforts in HR are based on telling people what they'll be *gaining* through change, rather than helping them feel better about what they'll *lose* (or what they might miss out on if they don't participate).

David Rock looks at this in a slightly different way with his SCARF model, which shows how our brains respond to threats automatically according to 'System One' thinking (in other words, we don't even know we're doing it). He identifies five losses we fear, and that lead us to behave 'badly':

- loss of status, which can lead to command-and-control leadership, for instance;

- loss of certainty, which creates an unwillingness to be open to new possibilities or ways of doing things;

---

[61] *Nudge: Improving Decisions About Health, Wealth and Happiness,* by Richard Thaler. Penguin, 2009, pp. 36–7.

- loss of autonomy, which can lead to the 'not invented here' syndrome;

- loss of relatedness, which means we're less likely to open up and collaborate when we're working with people we don't know;

- loss of fairness, which makes HR unwilling to move away from blanket systems and procedures, because we'd rather keep something that doesn't work than move to something that we worry may be unfair.

In summary these are the five elements of human psychology that underpin why we behave, think, and feel the way we do. We're predisposed to be more emotional than logical; we want to be like everyone else; we're lazy; we act according to habits; and we'd rather not lose something than gain a replacement that's more valuable. When you think about your failures and successes with change in the past, this will hopefully shed a ray of light on them.

You have to make change:

- appeal to people's emotions;

- seem as easy as possible;

- feel less scary than sticking with the status quo;

- appear worthwhile; and

- be desirable and normal.

Action point

- In your workbook, think of one time when you've tried and failed to get someone (or some people) to change. How many of these five human traits could you now apply to that situation, as a way of understanding where you went wrong? You can download your workbook here: https://disruptivehr.com/thehrchangetoolkitworkbook.

Quick recap

- Humans have five core traits which we need to work with, rather than against, if you want to initiate successful change:
  - o we're programmed to think emotionally rather than rationally;
  - o we want to be like everyone else;
  - o we're lazy and will do what's easiest;
  - o we do what we've always done; and
  - o we're more frightened of loss than excited by gain.

Lead Change the Human Way

I hope you've found your brief journey through some of the key elements of human psychology an interesting one. Here's where you start to apply it to leading change more easily and effectively than you've done before. After all, there's nothing more exhausting and demoralising than trying to force people to alter their way of working when they don't want to. If we in HR are serious about making a difference, we have to make it easy; we have to make it less scary; we have to make it feel worthwhile; and we have to make it seem desirable and normal.

This chapter will take you through how to achieve this, and in doing so I'm going to talk about nudge theory. This is a concept based on behavioural science, and indicates that positive reinforcement and indirect suggestions are more likely to influence the decision making of groups and individuals than instruction or enforcement. In other words, it recommends providing small, incremental encouragements to incentivise people to change, rather than implementing large-scale programmes that browbeat them into it. If you'd like to learn more about this area I suggest you read the bestselling book *Nudge*[62] by Richard Thaler, in which he outlines numerous tactics you can deploy. I'm going to focus on the key ones I feel

---

[62] *Nudge: Improving Decisions About Health, Wealth and Happiness,* by Richard Thaler. Penguin, 2009.

have a benefit for HR, giving you examples along the way.
In doing so I'll cover:

- why our default position is important;
- how reducing choice will help you;
- why the status quo isn't all bad (and what it has to do with habits);
- how it's not just what we say but the way we say it that matters;
- why timing is everything;
- how we can use the herd to our advantage;
- why small is better; and
- how to make change feel safe.

What's your default?

Going back to how intrinsically lazy we humans are, and how fond we are of doing what we've always done, it makes sense that when faced with a choice we typically plump for the default option. A classic example of this is automatic pension enrolment, which the UK Government introduced as a direct result of its Behavioural Insights Team's understanding of nudge theory. And it worked. Despite years of successive administrations explaining the benefits of contributing to a pension to a largely uninterested workforce, millions more Britons than before are now saving for retirement.[63] This is because automatic enrolment doesn't demand anything difficult from new employees. Instead of asking themselves, 'Should I join? How much will it cost? Why would I tax my

---

[63] https://www.theguardian.com/commentisfree/2017/oct/10/behavioural-economics-richard-thaler-nudge-nobel-prize-winner

brain with something so painful and boring?', they stick with the choice they've effectively already made.

Think about your default positions in HR. One approach you could try is to apply nudge theory to learning and development. At the moment, when we make decisions about who to invest training in, it's almost always those whom our nine-box grids tell us are the brightest and most ambitious. But what if your default standpoint was that growth wasn't optional? Instead of assuming people could only develop upwards with promotion, how about seeing it as something that could go sideways (moving around the company or extending a role), or deeper (becoming a stronger expert)? Everyone needs to develop and grow, and this works particularly well in companies with large numbers of long-serving employees who are experts in their field. These are the ones who often think learning isn't for them, with the danger they become stale and change-resistant. Your new default position would support greater agility, higher performance, and more innovation across the business, because no-one would be standing still or going backwards.

Recently I worked with a large, highly traditional public sector body. It was having trouble persuading its line managers to adopt flexible working practices because they were assumed to be unproductive. I suggested they changed their default position to one in which every job could be done flexibly, so if a manager thought one couldn't be they had to justify it; insisting a role could only be carried out during standard working hours would then become an active decision. Of course some still went down the old route, but it encouraged many to think differently. This shows how, by changing the default, you can use people's natural mental laziness to your advantage.

Challenge your own default settings

The other way you can make use of the power of the default is when you help people examine their own default thinking positions, including your own. We rarely overcome inertia without conscious effort, and this is shown in our habitual thinking and emotional patterns, which reveal themselves as unconscious biases in recruitment, talent-picking, and promotion. It's so much easier to assume somebody 'like us' is worthy of promotion or to be offered a job, than it is to consider someone who's different in gender, ethnicity, or social background.

The book *Inclusion Nudges*[64] by psychologists Tinna Neilsen and Lisa Kepinski looks at multiple nudges in relation to diversity, and their case studies are fascinating. For instance, the authors suggest that when you interview a job candidate you do so along with another interviewee and split the session into two parts. The first is a short, basic interview, after which you pause for a midway evaluation to check if you're resorting to your default thinking. You ask questions such as, 'Would we have thought the same if "he" was a "she", or if he'd got the same education as me?' or 'If he didn't have such a soft voice, would we have listened differently?' In this way you recognise your unconscious bias as your default position, and build in a challenge so as to achieve a better outcome.

We also tend to have default settings around the notion of treating people as adults in HR. Is yours that you don't trust people to behave in the right way? If it is, all your approaches will be based on this. If you assume

---

[64] *Inclusion Nudges Guidebook: Practical Techniques for Changing Behaviour, Culture & Systems to Mitigate Unconscious Bias and Create Inclusive Organisations*, by Tinna C. Neilsen and Lisa Kepinski. CreateSpace, 2016, pp. 136–7 and 165.

people are capable instead, you'll come at change from a positive angle and expect more from them.

Reduce the choice

In 2000 psychologists Sheena Lyengar and Mark Lepper carried out what's now become a well-known experiment[65] in which they set out 24 types of jam on a market stall, and the following day reduced this to six. Although the table with more choices attracted greater attention, when it came to purchasing the jam the sales on the 'six jam day' were ten times higher. This taps into what we know about taking the path of least resistance, and proves too much choice can be a bad thing. When we feel overloaded by an excessive number of options we're inclined to do nothing, rather than tax our brains with what seems to be a complicated decision. Instead of liberating us too much choice debilitates us.

Successful charities learned this long ago. Think of the last time you visited a charity website — you were probably presented with three different amounts you could donate. There were only three because the charity knew you didn't want to feel overwhelmed; they also made it easy by presenting you with a series of default amounts based on what others usually give. You can also see the influence of the herd mentality here. Maybe you intended to donate £5, but when you saw 'everyone else' was giving £25, you increased your donation.

In HR we need to offer options in a manner that makes it easy for people to choose. A classic way we often get this wrong is in the learning options we present. We feel good when we provide a Chinese takeaway menu of

---

[65] https://hbr.org/2006/06/more-isnt-always-better

training programmes covering every conceivable need, but what if we were only to offer one topic at a time, on a rolling basis? One month could be negotiation skills, and the next could be personal productivity. Employees would be more likely to take part in the training if that was all that was available, than if they had to choose what was right for them. In the realm of change, how could you make it easy for people by giving them a reduced range of options?

Protect the status quo

It might seem incongruous to advise you to protect the status quo when you want to ignite change, but what I'm focusing on here is how you position it as being okay to lose something. Remember when I talked about people being twice as worried about loss as they're excited by gain? For an HR practitioner trying to drive participation in a leadership development programme, for instance, this is important. What you've probably done in the past is to highlight the career opportunities your high potentials will *gain* by improving as a leader, but if you were to mention the opportunities they stand to *lose* by not taking part, you'd be putting it more persuasively.[66]

We're also more concerned with loss than gain in the way we protect our habits. Charles Duhigg, who I mentioned before, is an expert on habits and in his book *The Power of Habit*[67] he sees them as being less about patterns of behaviour and more about reward. According to his

---

[66] http://www.hrmagazine.co.uk/article-details/nudge–theory-in-hr-view-from-a-behavioural-economist

[67] *The Power of Habit: Why We Do What We Do, and How to Change*, by Charles Duhigg. Random House, 2013.

research, the reason they're so hard to break is that every habit has its prize; this tells your brain that your habit works well for you and is worth repeating. He gives the example from his own life of eating a chocolate bar at 3:00pm every day. Realising he'd put on weight and that it would be helpful to cut out his afternoon chocolate fix, he couldn't work out why it was so hard for him to resist. When he broke it down he realised the reward wasn't only from the bar itself, but from the way it made him get up from his desk in the afternoon and chat to people in the work canteen while he was buying it. He realised he could still do the moving around and chatting without buying the chocolate, and it became easier to break the habit because he was still receiving the same rewards.

This shows that if you want someone to change their behaviour — in other words, to break a habit and form a new one — you have to identify the kickback they get from it and either recreate it differently or provide it through a new route; any new behaviour has to have the same reward as the old one. People's reward hierarchy differs from person to person, but it's not hard to take a guess at what the payback is for them. For instance, I'm sure you've seen managers blocking their talent from transferring to other teams even when they know that it would be better for the organisation as a whole. But think about it. If that manager receives a bonus for their own team's work, and praise for having a low staff turnover, why would they want to let that person go? How about if you changed the feedback so it rewarded their generosity instead? You could even take this a step further: your new default position could be that 'Our best leaders are net exporters of talent'. If that was your starting point, you'd begin to question why somebody had a high retention rate in their team — it wouldn't automatically be seen as positive.

Frame the change

The way in which we present information can alter its perceived meaning, so it seems less threatening and more attractive. The phrase 'performance review', for instance, sounds intimidating and retrospective and therefore non-value-adding, whereas a 'frequent check-in' or 'career conversation' sounds more positive. If I were to hear my review described like that, I'd assume something helpful and supportive would come of it.

The authors of *Inclusion Nudges* give the example of HR's perennial struggle to make leadership teams more diverse. Although we mean well, when we incentivise leaders to recruit more women and minority groups by setting target percentage levels, this triggers leaders' unconscious default associations about diversity being a 'nice to have' rather than a necessity. Whereas if we were to frame the request differently we could present it as something that would improve performance, which is to everyone's benefit. So we'd say, 'We want no more than 70 percent of our leadership team to be homogeneous.' That's coming at it from a different angle, isn't it? We're being clear now that homogeneity is bad for business, and that by increasing diversity we're reducing it. It's less threatening.

Prime the change

Priming has some overlap with framing but is more to do with timing than language. It's a way of helping people approach choices in a prepared state, by enabling them to visualise a viewpoint or feeling before they make their decision. It's easier to understand this through an example. One of the problems we in HR often have is

with managers not doing a good enough job of the induction process. You know the scenario: the new starter arrives, but their boss is so busy they haven't given a
moment's thought to welcoming them, so the hapless
recruit spends their first few days reading the induction
manual and wondering if they should ask for their old
job back. The traditional HR solution to this is to assume
we can't trust managers to do induction well, and to take
it over with our painfully boring and officious induction
programmes.

Let's look at what Google does instead. It set up an
automatic process whereby an email goes to the line manager of a new starter the night before the recruit is due to
join, asking the manager to remember what it felt like on
their first day and to think about what kind of experience
they'd want their new person to have. This primes those
managers to make the right decision at exactly the right
time.

Another way you could make use of priming is when
you want to encourage more frequent performance conversations. You could do a quick video of what one looks
like, so when people come to do their own they already
understand how it works. Or you could send a reminder
to employees to ask for a career conversation with their
boss and include some questions they might want to ask.
By modelling or prompting what you want people to do
in advance you make it easy for them to imagine themselves doing the new thing, which in turn makes it more
likely to happen.

Follow the herd

You learned about how humans instinctively conform
with others in their 'herd' in the last chapter, and you

can tap into this trait in order to lead change. There are two ways of doing this.

Position the option you want people to take as the one the majority are already doing

If you want to encourage more managers to carry out frequent check-ins instead of annual performance reviews, how about announcing that 80 percent of top performing managers have already chosen to do this? This positions it as something all managers want to be part of. In fact, I think we should be braver about making the desired option seem like becoming a member of an exclusive club.

Instead of struggling to persuade laggards to comply with a new process, exclude them by default

We need to be more bullish about this in HR. I once worked with a client who wanted to introduce a spot reward system, whereby managers would be given a budget and the ability to distribute gifts to people at the moment they did something great. This took advantage of the fact that rewards work best when they're surprising, personalised, and timely. The HR Director was concerned, though: 'What about the ones who won't do it because they forget, or because they're nervous about not having detailed rules to follow?' she said. I could see her point, because we all know there are managers who either don't care about motivating their people, or who are so anxious about getting it wrong they can't countenance not having any rules to blame for their mistakes.

But what I said was, 'Well, just tell them if they don't feel comfortable doing it without rules, they don't have to take part at all. The managers who participate will receive the budgets, and they won't. Get tougher with them, because they won't want to be excluded.' Can you imagine being one of those '10 percent' managers, and having to explain to your team that the reason others have been receiving boxes of chocolates and trips out is because there aren't enough rules? When we think about it like that the answer's obvious, but what we tend to do instead is either avoid implementing the change at all because we can't get every manager to agree to it, or indulge those who want the rules and create them — thereby making the process a pain in the backside for everyone else.

Shrink the change

Why do businesses have an obsession with big being better? At the BBC we instigated a change programme called Delivering Quality First (DQF), which felt (and was) massive, with multiple project streams and five-year time horizons. These huge projects are always difficult and scary for everyone and encourage our elephant and chimp brains to kick in with fearful thoughts. If we want leaders to change willingly we have to shrink the size of the challenge they face.

Much of my thinking in this area comes from the brilliant book *Switch*, which I mentioned in the last chapter. The authors assert that if we can find a way to make something seem small or even temporary, we'll find it easier to persuade people to do it. This is the thinking behind Alcoholics Anonymous, which encourages its members to give up drink one day at a time, not forever. That way drinkers aren't tempted to give up before they've even started ('How will I cope at Christmas? Or at my sister's wedding? Or when I get my test results?'). AA gives them a 'Just for Today' card which reads: 'Just for today I will try to live through this day only, and not tackle all my problems at once. I can do something for 12 hours that would appall me if I felt that I had to keep it up for a lifetime.'

I'm also a devotee of a technique called the 'Five Minute Room Rescue' by home-organising guru Marla Cilley. When cleaning the entire house seems like such a mountainous task we decide not to bother, we can set a kitchen timer for five minutes and just tackle the worst room. When the buzzer goes, we can stop with a clear conscience. This taps into the notion that getting going is often the hardest part of change because it feels so daunting, but that anyone can accomplish something useful in five minutes and do it again the next day. Our confidence grows as we discover it's not so difficult after all, and we want to do more of it.

We can use this in HR when we want people to change their habits. Instead of asking leaders to have on-going conversations with their staff each day, we could suggest they have one weekly five-minute conversation with a couple of their people by their desk, and to comment on one good thing that week. Just one five-minute conversation, and one comment — give it a go. Western Union did this when it wanted its leaders to improve their way of managing talent. Instead of the standard nine-box grid accompanied by endless calibration discussions, it asked clusters of managers to come together for an hour a month to talk about the talent in their teams. It shrunk an industrial-scale task into a human-sized one.

Another way of minimising a challenge is to break it down into staged tasks. The educational technique of 'scaffolding' takes this approach. It states that, instead of assuming teachers need to teach something sizeable such as how to do algebra in one go, they take the end point and break it down into chunks. Each chunk involves learning something new, but messing up one of them won't put the learner off doing the rest of it. For instance, if you were to try to hold line managers responsible for making pay and bonus decisions rather than it being controlled centrally in HR, this would be a terrifying prospect for most leaders because they'd assume managers would bust the salary budget in no time. However, your starting point in HR could be that instead of not implementing this change for fear of it causing problems, you could do it in stages like this:

1. Ask the managers to carry out a theoretical exercise on how they would go about the task. Give feedback to help them.
2. Feed in some example tricky situations and discuss how they'd respond.
3. Let them try it with the lowest risk elements of their team, and to reflect with you afterwards on how it went.
4. Keep doing this until you have them off their water wings and swimming independently.

This might sound time consuming, but how many hours do you spend carrying out the annual pay review at the moment? With scaffolding, you protect people from making huge mistakes and losing their confidence, creating ways for them to practise and improve.

Make it okay for managers to try something new

Even when we see the value in a change of behaviour the combination of our herd mentality, our concern about loss of status, and our System One thinking can prevent us from even trying. It's no wonder, because organisations bang on about accountability all the time. What they really mean is, 'Who can we blame if it doesn't work?'

It goes without saying that in order to deliver HR in new ways, we're dependent upon leaders trying new methods: facilitating peer reviews rather than telling their teams how they're performing; holding open conversations instead of giving someone a grade; and owning decisions about pay and reward. We ask them to put their confidence, reputation, and self-esteem on the line. That's pretty scary. If we're going to help them trust that it's okay to change, we need to create a climate of psychological safety which makes it comfortable for them to experiment.

In her book *Mindset: The New Psychology of Success*,[68] Dr Carol Dweck explains that our behaviours are determined by how we see ourselves. If we have a fixed mindset we believe our qualities are set in stone; intelligence and personality are fixed traits rather than ones that can be developed. This is why some leaders say, 'I'm too old to change. This is who I am. I've always been like this.' The problem with having a fixed mindset is that it creates an urgency to prove ourselves over and over again, with criticism being received as an attack on our character and to be avoided at all costs. A growth mindset, on the other hand, comes from the belief that our basic qualities can be cultivated through learning and effort. Obviously people differ greatly in their attitudes, talents, interests, and temperaments, but we can all improve through application and experience. When we believe we can do this we're driven to learn, practice, give things a go, and to see criticism as valuable feedback that should be embraced. In fact, the hallmark of a growth mindset is a passion for sticking at worthwhile pursuits, especially when they're not going well.

---

[68] *Mindset: The New Psychology of Success*, by Dr Carol Dweck. Ballantine, 2007.

We need to help our leaders develop a growth mindset, because otherwise they won't feel safe enough to experiment with change.

How can HR help leaders to develop this growth mindset? There are various ways.

Recognise there isn't one right way of leading

This is where traditional leadership competency frameworks are so unhelpful, because they point to a set of behaviours that people either possess or don't. They also suggest there's only one way of leading, because the frameworks typically describe the 'perfect leader', whereas we know leaders need to vary their style depending on their situation. There are times when command-and-control can be helpful, for instance in a short crisis period, but we continue to look for extrovert leadership even though it's perfectly possible to be an introvert and a great leader. We need to encourage leaders to find ways of delivering the outputs we want but in ways that work for them.

Encourage leaders to share

Suggest your leaders get together regularly and share how things are going for them (you'll need to prime a couple in advance to relate their stories). This will give them the opportunity to learn from one another. The meetings aren't for boasting, but for them to discuss where they've messed up and even to have a laugh about it. A major bank holds a brown bag lunch every month to talk about talent; simply gathering together every few weeks to share highs and lows encourages leaders to learn and become better.

Celebrate those who've worked hard at leadership even if the results weren't good

This feels counterintuitive, and puts me in mind of the funny film *Talladega Nights*. In this, Will Ferrell's ultra-competitive dad constantly yells at him with the challenge: 'If you're not first, you're last!' But if you celebrate effort, you foster the factors that help leaders to grow. You also make it safe for them to try new things in order to improve, because your focus is on their good work and not on their results. One way of doing this is to encourage well-respected leaders to share their fallibility; the more those who are perceived as great can talk about their mistakes, the better. We don't celebrate leadership effort enough, and in more macho circles this is even seen as weak. Some companies are even experimenting with rewarding failure as it's such an intrinsic part of innovation. Without failure, we're not evolving.

In all this, remember the 90/10 rule you want to avoid. Start with the leaders who already have a growth mindset and who are curious, even if they're currently your harshest critics. Then build a movement gradually — don't try to persuade all your leaders at once. You can't compensate for those who have no interest in being an effective people leader.

Action point

- In your workbook, take each way of making change easier from the bullet points at the beginning and apply it to one major change you've tried and failed with in the past. How would you do them differently now? You can download your workbook here: https://disruptivehr.com/thehrchangetoolkitworkbook.

Quick recap

- Effective and lasting change can only happen when you go with the grain of human nature, instead of forcing it on people against their will.

- There are eight main ways of leading change that take human psychology into account:

  o setting new default positions;

  o reducing choice;

  o making it easy to change habits;

  o framing the change positively;

  o priming people for change to get them ready;

  o positioning change as something everyone's doing;

  o making change feel small; and

  o encouraging a growth mindset in leaders.

Empower Your Front Line

Clearly, influencing leaders and line managers is a vital task because by persuading them to lead, manage, engage, reward, and communicate differently, you'll spread change more widely and quickly than if you were only to work with the individuals below them. However, you also have the challenge of bringing change to the rest of your organisation directly, and this involves influencing your front-line staff. All the tactics I outlined for leaders and line managers in the previous chapter still apply, but here I'll suggest some additional ideas for helping to change behaviour at scale. It'll feel like you're conducting a whole orchestra instead of a band.

Reduce the rules

Central to empowering your front line is reducing the number of rules you ask people to follow. Rules drive compliance, but they can also stifle innovation and rarely help employees develop greater agility in coping with change. On the contrary, they make them more likely to wait for permission instead. The problem is, we find this difficult in HR. We're keen to try new things but we're loathe to give up the innumerable policies, rules, and processes we've worked so hard to create. Even when we see how unhelpful they are, we tell ourselves a tweak here and a change there will be sufficient because stripping a chunk of them away feels too risky.

If this is you, I sympathise. However, there are two key benefits to reducing the number of rules your employees have to follow. The first is when you reduce constraints you free people to think and behave differently (and better). The second is it's incredibly hard for people to feel encouraged to try new things if there's a rule keeping them where they are. When I work with HR Directors who are removing performance reviews, for instance, I often find they hang onto certain parts of the annual cycle such as objective setting and personal bonuses, making it harder to move onto something more fluid; it's like they're stuck in an annual mindset rut. This goes back to humans feeling twice as reluctant to lose something as they're excited to gain a replacement.

Gary Hamel's book *What Matters Now*[69] contains a fascinating analysis of organisational change at scale. He's a passionate critic of bureaucracy, seeing it as preventing organisations from adapting in a rapidly changing world, and even has a way of calculating a company's BMI[70] (Bureaucracy Mass Index). In his view bureaucracy must die, and I'll give the most relevant reasons for HR here.[71]

- It *creates friction* by forcing people with fresh ideas to run a multi-level gauntlet of approval, thereby creating a time lag.

- It *distorts decisions* because it gives too much power to senior executives, who tend to be more invested in legacy systems than their younger counterparts.

[69] *What Matters Now: How to Win in a World of Relentless Change, Ferocious Competition, and Unstoppable Innovation,* by Gary Hamel. Wiley, 2012.

[70] https://hbr.org/2017/05/assessment-do-you-know-how-bureaucratic-your-organization-is

[71] http://fortune.com/2014/03/26/why-bureaucracy-must-die/

- It *discourages dissent*, making it difficult for subordinates to speak up.

- It *misdirects competition* by encouraging people to jostle for promotion and political advantage.

- It *thwarts innovation* by over-weighting experience and under-weighting unconventional thinking.

- It *hobbles initiative* by throwing up barriers to risk taking.

- It *obliterates nuance* by centralising too many decisions and demanding compliance with uniform rules and procedures.

I think this is a brilliant summary of what's wrong with overly heavy bureaucracy, and you can see how it links back to the Adult part of my EACH model: treating employees as adults rather than children. But how can you go about reducing the rules in a way that's easiest for you? There are eight key ways:

- start small and ask your employees;

- keep them informed;

- treat front-line staff like adults;

- crowdsource ideas from outside HR;

- find the bright spots;

- see large companies as a group of smaller units;

- discover your micro influencers; and

- create a movement of change.

Start small and ask the employees

You would probably feel nervous about the idea of doing away with rules entirely, but that's not what I'm suggesting. Don't sweep away a rule overnight that might cause issues with, for instance, your major regulator or with health and safety. I advise you to start with minor, low-risk changes to the guidelines that frustrate your people the most and prevent them from doing a good job; in fact, it's surprisingly easy to change small rules quickly. TD Bank, for instance, offered $50 to any member of staff who spotted a rule that was getting in the way of providing a good service to its customers.

How can you discover which rules are preventing your employees from doing their best work? One of our clients carried out a survey outside its staff canteen; the constraint that came up time and again was the lack of flexible working hours, so that's what it decided to focus on first. Try not to prioritise the rules that matter most to you, but those that your front-line staff see as the biggest barrier to excellent customer service.

Keep people informed

Gary Hamel also points out we need to provide more insight and data to our front-line staff than we currently do. Senior leaders receive huge amounts of financial figures and sales data, but the front line rarely gets anything granular enough to help them make choices about what they might do differently. I'm not suggesting you overwhelm employees with endless information, but I do remember my frustration at the BBC when I wanted to gain suggestions about how to make major money savings. The only data our front-line staff had ever seen was the annual report, which didn't give the right level of detail. Why didn't we feel we could share the same information with them that the senior people had? Those who were interested would have seen it as a useful prompt to think about how they could do things differently, and instead of sending them on endless productivity programmes, or centralising cost-saving decisions and cascading them down, we could have been enabling them to generate the insights themselves.

Treat front-line staff like adults

Gary Hamel gives a brilliant example of how technology company Adobe empowers its rank and file employees. The company realised an individual on the front line could have a great idea to raise productivity or improve customer service, but that when they took it to their line manager they'd be told to write a business case which would be cascaded up the various levels of approval. Unsurprisingly most staff found this demotivating. Adobe removed this barrier by creating an open-source innovation process it called Adobe Kickbox,[72] which does two interesting things. First, any employee can apply for it so there's no permission involved; applicants receive a downloadable training resource, giving them the tools to take an idea from concept to implementation themselves. Secondly, it gives each applicant a credit card loaded with $1,000 to fund their idea; for instance, they might want to set up focus group research or develop a quick prototype. How about that for treating front-line staff as adults? Instead of passing their bright idea onto the 'grown-ups' to handle it, they're trusted to do it themselves. What's more, there are no questions asked — the only justification employees have to give is to share what they learned, not whether it succeeded or failed, and this encourages a growth mindset. So far about 1,000 people have taken advantage: that's $1,000,000 spent on empowering employees to innovate, with some significant changes as a result.

I love the example of Adobe Kickbox, but on a smaller scale here's an idea that CRM company HubSpot came

---

[72] https://kickbox.adobe.com/

up with: if you think you can learn something from some-body, you can take them out for lunch on your expens-es — no questions asked. This encourages employees to take charge of their own learning, because HubSpot trusts that people know what they need to improve on. I'm sure there is the odd rogue who treats himself or her-self and a friend to a cheeky free lunch, but remember we're not designing policies for the 10 percent. We're de-signing them for the majority, with the assumption that people will use them well.

Crowdsource your ideas from outside HR

This is an area in which I'm seeing more and more ac-tivity. Currently it's most apparent in HR departments in the technology sector because they already have a sound understanding of it, but I've got a feeling it will soon spread to others. It's the concept of a hackathon, which uses an aspect of design thinking to enable HR to see its services through employees' eyes. These events are fast-paced, taking a day or at most a week, and generate multiple ideas by bringing in diverse thinkers with their own perspectives. So instead of us in HR sitting in a room and coming up with the changes we think are essential, we facilitate a hackathon involving employees, internal business leaders, people in HR, software designers, prod-uct researchers, marketers, and anyone else who thinks differently.

LinkedIn held a hackathon for interns from various Silicon Valley firms with the aim of improving employee engagement. Cisco closed its HR department for 24 hours in order to hold a 'breakathon', which gave birth to 105 new HR solutions.[73] And DBS Bank wanted to enhance

---

[73] https://business.linkedin.com/talent-solutions/blog/hr/2016/how-hackathons-can-help-you-re-imagine-hr

its employee experience by using automated intelligence and robotics; within 12 hours employees had generated over 200 solutions. This led to its HR team introducing a robot called Harri who answered routine questions using a chat box.[74]

I love the notion of HR not having to be the one to come up with all the ideas, but being the facilitator and contributor instead. How might holding a hackathon change your approach to talent, performance management, and induction?

Find the bright spots

Another way of speeding up change by crowdsourcing from your front line comes from Chip and Dan Heath's book *Switch*. In this they point out that when we're managing large-scale change we tend to do a huge amount of analysis of what's wrong so we can fill the gap: in other words, a deficit-based analysis. But what works better is to find the bright spots, or what's working well, and to extract insights from them. This enables you to focus your attention, and is a quicker and more effective way of creating change. At the BBC we carried out a review on bullying and harassment in the organisation. But instead of spending all our time examining any unpleasant activities going on we also asked people, 'Who are the leaders you love working for?' Around 50 names came up repeatedly, and we asked the employees what it was they did that was so special. Interestingly, the answers were based on being better humans rather than being technical specialists or great communicators; it was all about humility. 'They know my name.' 'I have a good connection with them.'

---

[74] https://www.forbes.com/sites/jeannemeister/2017/09/27/the-future-of-work-hr-hackathons-improve-the-candidate-and-employee-experience/

'They say sorry when they've got something wrong.' 'They give me credit for my work.' Two particular leaders stood out: Tim Davy and Peter Salmon. Both were highly visible to front-line employees, spending huge amounts of time visiting groups of managers and staff and talking about why change was needed. Peter Salmon, for instance, led the successful opening of BBC MediaCity in Salford, the first new BBC centre outside of London for decades. Looking at what those leaders did right, rather than getting bogged down in what all the others did wrong, was a quicker and more effective way of working out how to encourage all leaders to improve.

Break up large companies into smaller units

In 2005, Chinese home appliance manufacturer Haier divided itself into 2,000 highly autonomous profit centres, splitting thousands of employees into micro-enterprise units each focusing on a single appliance or service.[75] It called it the Rendanheyi Model: 'ren' refers to each employee, 'dan' to the needs of each user, and 'heyi' to the connection between the employee and the need. What this company recognised was that large organisations are incredibly hard to change, which is why startups are so much more agile and responsive than their monolithic counterparts. While one could question how a large business could retain its economies of scale when split into smaller factions, Haier is a hugely successful company and decided if it was to compete with startup competitors that were out to steal its market share, it had better go some way towards replicating what they looked and felt like.

---

[75] http://www.haier.net/en/about_haier/news/201703/
t20170328_345989.shtml

Clearly, it's not always possible for HR to break up a business into smaller parts, but if you start thinking about your company in terms of being multiple business units rather than a monolithic entity, it will help you instigate change in your front line in a more agile way.

Discover your micro influencers

Over Christmas I was chatting with a friend who works in marketing for a large pharmaceutical company. She was lamenting her difficulties with recruiting micro social media influencers in her product's target market. I'm sure you've heard about brands using famous celebrities with huge social followings to promote products, but my friend's dilemma points to a newer trend, which is for businesses to work with *micro* influencers — typically people who have 50,000 followers rather than millions. The idea is to build a network of these smaller influencers, who despite their relative unknown status still have fantastic networks, and to send them products in exchange for reviews. Because these people aren't big name stars, they're trusted by their audience.

Let's think about how you can use micro influencers. I'm sure you're aware it's good practice to know who in your organisation is well networked, and that there are certain people in your front line who are the most trusted and well liked. But do these influencers know about what you're trying to achieve, and are they willing to share it? If, for instance, you want to change annual performance reviews to career conversations, how could you work with them to help bed this in? If you think about it, for them to share a credible story about change they need to have access to the same intelligence, insights, and stories as you do. It's not a question of giving them a brief and asking them to talk about it, but of providing them with the information and encouragement to use their networks the way they see best. By doing this you're building a change platform rather than a change programme,[76] making large-scale collaboration easier and more effective. You're also equipping your micro influencers with the key messages *and* collateral to help with recruitment; one third of candidates rank current employees as the most credible source of information.[77]

Create a movement

Your front line may contain hundreds or even thousands of people, so let's look at some of the large-scale social movements that have arisen over the years and ask how they could apply to what you're trying to achieve. We know top-down, command-and-control change that comes from a centralised HR function isn't nearly as effective as that which springs from an organisation's employees, so how can you create the conditions in which a movement could arise?

All effective movements start with emotions rather than facts. Encouraging your people to engage with a problem that's frustrating them, rather than feeding them statistics about what the issues are, will always work best (think of the #MeToo movement as an example). Start small and build from the ground up, recognising it's not going to be a top-down process. This means taking a bit of a risk; for instance, would you be happy to share the negative results of your staff survey with everyone?

Harnessing networks that already exist is a vital piece of this. The leaders of the 1960s US civil rights movement recruited members through the church network,

---

[76] https://www.mckinsey.com/business-functions/organization/our-insights/build-a-change-platform-not-a-change-program

[77] http://www.manpowergroupsolutions.co.uk/wp-content/uploads/2016/05/BrandDetectives.pdf

because this was well established and populated by those who felt ready for change. Every organisation has its networks, including those on social media. Yours could be diversity groups, social groups, or millennials groups. Do you know what they are, and are you accessing and communicating with them?

As a final point, front-line staff are notoriously sceptical when leaders waffle on about change rather than walking the talk. In an interesting article in the *Harvard Business Review*,[78] Bryan Walker and Sarah A. Soule recommend creating a 'movement, not a mandate'. They give the example of Indian pharmaceutical company Dr Reddy's, which came up with the agile purpose of 'Good health can't wait'. But instead of putting this in mission statements and plastering it over its office walls, it decided to use it to guide all its decision making; in other words, to 'do' the idea rather than talk about it.

---

[78] https://hbr.org/2017/06/changing-company-culture-requires-a-movement-not-a-mandate

Action point

- In your workbook, think of three ways you could discover which rules to ditch or change by talking to your front-line staff. You can download your workbook here: https://disruptivehr.com/thehrchangetoolkitworkbook.

Quick recap

- Influencing change among large groups of people requires different techniques than with small groups of leaders and managers.
- There are eight key ways to do this:
  o start small and ask your employees;
  o keep people informed;
  o treat front-line staff like adults;
  o crowdsource ideas from outside HR;
  o find the bright spots;
  o break up large companies into smaller units;
  o discover your micro influencers; and
  o create a movement.

Pilot Your Change

Now you understand the best ways to influence change, it's time to look at the change itself. How does it feel to you? Your answer will depend on whether you see it as something you can deal with in bite-sized chunks or as a huge, scary task with lots of risks attached. As you'll have gathered by now there's nothing speedy or safe about making waves in HR, but that's not to say there aren't ways of launching your change that are less hazardous and stressful than what you're probably used to. Chief among them is the practice of piloting your change before you launch it in full.

Piloting is not something we do enough of in HR; when I consult with clients who want help implementing HR change, it amazes me how rarely they consider running a pilot before they dive in. I worked with a utility company recently; it had 10,000 employees and decided to remove all performance ratings and bonuses in one go. That was far too risky! I get the impression that in the enthusiasm of implementing a new process or system people are desperate to leap into it immediately so as not to spoil the momentum, rather than taking what seems like the unnecessary step of trying it out on a small group first. There's also something in our HR psyche about the importance of changing things consistently and perfectly for everybody, which works against the notion of a pilot. We want our services to be flawless and loved by all, which means the notion of testing the water with an imperfect version first can feel wrong.

There are various problems with this 'all or nothing' approach, the main one of which is that, despite the extensive pre-consultation processes beloved by HR, there's no way of us knowing for sure whether or not a change is going to work without trying it out. If we launch something new based on guesswork and assumptions, we're only ever going to use our own judgement to decide if it's good enough, and it's not our judgement that matters most — it's that of our users.

What's a pilot? It's a way of testing your new service with a sub-group of the people you eventually envisage using it. Piloting is an incredibly useful step in the roll-out process because it means you can iron out any issues before everyone climbs on board. As such, it has some elements in common with the prototyping I talked about in the 'How Product Designers Do It' chapter, in that it enables you iterate and improve your service before it's 'finalised' (if indeed it ever is). However, piloting is less rough and ready than prototyping, because it involves testing a relatively polished version of the end product or service in a real-life scenario.

How to run a pilot

Piloting is pretty straightforward as long as you approach it in a systematic way. Here are the steps to take.

1. *Create a hypothesis*

   What are you testing? An example of a hypothesis could be, 'Simplifying our expenses policy will result in higher user satisfaction and a lowering of expenses claims'. Make sure you can measure the results of your pilot according to your hypothesis.

2. *Choose a sub-section of your end-user base that you can get your arms around*

Here's a helpful example of how I ran a pilot when I was at the BBC. We were exploring the idea of offering employees unlimited holiday leave instead of restricting them to a set number of weeks a year. Clearly there was no way we could have implemented this in one go across the organisation, so we decided to pilot the change in the Natural History Unit. Why did we choose this department? It was the perfect size as a proportion of the whole (around 250 people), it was located away from the main London office which made it a safer place to try something radical, and it had a leader who was curious to see how it could work and 'got' the concept. This is essential. The leader you choose doesn't have to be the best in your business to be a good fit for a pilot, but they do have to be happy to experiment.

3. *Create a control group*

You need to compare the results from your treatment group (the people you're piloting with) and a similar group who don't receive the pilot. If possible keep your control and treatment groups within the same business area, as it's easier for comparative purposes. You don't have to have a lot of people in each group — I gave the example of 250 people but you might have 10 if that's a sensible number for you; this isn't a scientific experiment, but simply a way of measuring your results so you can discover what works. Also, try to avoid making any changes to your control group during the experiment.

4. *Design your experiment*

Keep the number of things you're testing relatively low. You're not wanting to change everything, only to pilot one or two elements of your hypothesis. Suppose you want to change your performance management process: you could have a control group in which you change nothing, and two treatment groups. In one of those treatment groups you could pilot team and peer reviews; in another you could try frequent check-ins and no grades. This means you're really testing two changes, not four, because the two alternatives are grouped together. Your hypothesis might be that moving to peer reviews is a more effective way for people to evaluate their performance, and that if you move to check-ins you'll improve the quality of the conversation. The main thing is that you're managing it in a clear and controlled way.

5. *Run your pilot*

During the activity of the experiment, regularly compare your control and treatment groups to test your hypothesis. Don't leave it until the end to find out what happened — if you don't talk to them briefly at least every week you'll miss out on valuable data because people will forget what happened. They'll also feel less motivated if they're not sure you're interested in the outcome.

Your pilot should also be relatively short and simple because otherwise people will get tired of it. Sometimes I see pilots lasting a year, by the end of which everyone's lost interest. Or they include seven or eight changes, which is unmanageable; you won't be able to draw any sensible conclusions from that. I worked with a manufacturing company recently in which piloting was a new concept for the HR Director. In the end we planned to recruit three teams on which to test one of our ideas; one was peer reviews, one was frequent check-ins, and the other was getting the team leaders together to have regular talent conversations about their people. It was set to run for between one and three months — perfect.

I hope you can see the value of piloting now. It means when you go live with your new process you'll already understand the capability gaps you need to fill and how people are likely to respond to it, so you can market it more effectively. You'll also have ironed out most of the wrinkles so everyone will enjoy using it and find it beneficial.

Action point

- In your workbook, pick one new significant transformation you have planned in. How could you pilot it rather than going live with a mass roll-out? Who could you pilot it with? And what process would you use? You can download your workbook here: https://disruptivehr.com/thehrchangetoolkitworkbook.

Quick recap

- Piloting change is an under-used concept in HR, but has numerous benefits:
  - o it reveals what needs changing before everyone uses a new process;
  - o it enables you to market it more effectively because you have feedback; and
  - o it makes change less scary for everyone.
- To run a pilot:
  - o create a hypothesis;
  - o form treatment and control groups;
  - o design your experiment; and
  - o run your pilot.

Brand and Launch Your Change

When I remember some of the HR initiatives I've launched over the years, I feel like hiding my head in my hands. Full-scale, blanket roll-outs, accompanied by Q & As, policy documents, training manuals, endless forms, and multiple elements of paperwork, they were probably some of the dullest launches on earth. It didn't occur to me I was marketing something, or should be persuading people that the change was worth participating in — I just thought if it was there, they would come. I've learned a lot since then, and much of it has been from my fellow professionals in marketing and advertising. In this chapter I'll take some of their techniques and strategies for launching products with impact, and show how these can help our thinking in HR.

There are various elements to a successful launch:

- naming your service with your target audience in mind;
- gaining permission from the right people to promote it;
- creating and distributing a constant stream of helpful content; and
- managing a rolling launch instead of a one-push promotion.

Name your service

What's in a name? Plenty, as it happens. However, we don't always feel comfortable with giving our initiatives appealing and direct names in HR, do we? Maybe we dismiss it as PR spin or worry we'll look disingenuous with a catchy name. This is simply because we're not used to it. We're trained to be accurate and to avoid potential discrimination claims, instead of focusing on how we can appeal to people. These legal concerns about accuracy are understandable, but in the vast majority of cases are unfounded — it's just a habit we've got into. Let's put ourselves 'out there' with confidence and, when we name a change, ask ourselves, 'Is this something I would feel attracted to if all I knew about it was the name?' After all, we're end users ourselves and know what appeals to us, so let's use this insight when we do the launching too.

What kind of naming works best? We know in the consumer world people remember names they can understand quickly and that are impactful and memorable. In their book *Positioning*,[79] Al Ries and Jack Trout point out that 'Newsweek' is a clever name because it does what it says on the tin, it's short, and everyone gets it. What we tend to do when we name an initiative or new service in HR, however, is to come up with acronyms, or to create names based on accurate descriptions, rather being appealing. We need to change this by considering our audience.

As I mentioned before, the term 'career conversations' both accurately describes what the process is and infers its essence. 'Check-ins' is another name I like because it makes having quick, regular catch-ups appear

---

[79] *Positioning: The Battle for Your Mind*, by Al Ries and Jack Trout. McGraw-Hill Education, 2001.

easy and manageable. And instead of an 'employee handbook' could we call it a 'welcome pack'? I love Virgin Trains' reward programme's name, which is 'You're Amazing'. This brings attention to its reward and recognition element and also ties in beautifully with its consumer brand. The 'Virgin Trains Benefits Programme', on the other hand, would sound like some kind of social security plan.

I came across another brilliant example of naming recently. A marketing agency wanted to run seminars for its people about pension changes in the business. Its HR team decided to go with something more interesting than the usual pension names ('Plan For Your Future'), and instead put up posters of the actor Sean Penn which said, 'Keep saying this actor's name over and over and what do you get?' Try it! Then they said, 'If you want to hear more about this, come to the seminar.' The agency's people loved it and it caused a real stir.

Gain permission to market your change

Permission marketing has the twin benefits of finding out what people want and of enabling you to spread your message to those who are keen to listen. It's a growing trend in social media marketing, and one of the key thinkers in this area is marketing guru Seth Godin, whose book *Permission Marketing*[80] is an excellent read. He explains how advertising in the past was interruptive, with messages bombarding people on TV, in print media, and on billboards. What he advocates instead is to gradually build

---

[80] *Permission Marketing: Turning Strangers Into Friends and Friends Into Customers*, by Seth Godin. Simon & Schuster UK, 2007.

up a relationship with your target users by asking their permission to give them more information; by doing this, you create a database of willing and interested people. The starting point is therefore to gain the permission of your employees to be told about your launch, not to assume they'll all be interested. This fits well with what I've mentioned previously about being led by your end users instead of implementing a one-size-fits-all solution.

Permission marketing also gives you valuable data. If people say they want to know more about your approach to learning, for instance, or your new reward or induction processes, you can identify them as early adopters. These will be useful to you when you want to pilot your change, or for user research. You're building a relationship with those who want to learn more, rather than annoying everybody when they might not be interested. Remember, all departments have their initiatives, and we can easily forget that the employees on the receiving end of a blanket communication from HR have also received ten times this number from the rest of the organisation. Permission marketing is respectful of people's time and energy and also, being user-led, treats employees as adults and consumers. We could certainly do with more of this in HR.

Develop a stream of helpful content

Content marketing is a phrase you'll no doubt have heard of. It means instead of broadcasting messages to your employees, you provide them with a stream of insightful content to help them to do their jobs more effectively. It's useful because not only does it deliver information that's appreciated by its consumers but it also fosters trust in, and appreciation of, HR; we instinctively want to reciprocate when someone helps us. Although

I'm talking about content marketing here in the context of launching something new, it doesn't have to be limited to that — it can be an ongoing process. You're positioning HR as the people who understand how to lead, manage, and do great work, which means when you do launch something your audience is predisposed to pay attention to it. I remember when I worked as an HR Director, leaders around my business would often circulate links to interesting articles they'd come across. Through this they showed they were well read and had a breadth of understanding that went further than them simply getting their job done; this helped build their credibility. Then when they spoke about an issue, people were more likely to listen because they had authority.

Content marketing can also spark interest in your initiative by tapping into what people want to know more about, as well as avoiding the usual scenario of HR telling people what to do. It can work for the driest of subjects, too. In his book *Epic Content Marketing*[81] Joe Pulizzi gives an example of an agricultural technology company selling farming machinery. It decided to produce a sales catalogue, but instead of simply featuring its products it also included interesting articles about the latest industry developments and called it 'The Furrow'. Because it provided trustworthy advice that was appreciated by its readers, sales increased.

How could you use this in HR? For instance, you might want to market a new training programme for leaders. If you were to provide irresistible content about leadership, that would be an excellent way of getting their attention. You could use great TED talks, articles written by HR or

---

[81] *Epic Content Marketing: How to Tell a Different Story, Break through the Clutter, and Win More Customers by Marketing Less*, by Joe Pulizzi. McGraw-Hill Education, 2013.

externally, a review of a book on leadership that's just been published, and multiple other pieces of content.

Linked to this is how you can use content marketing to make your business more attractive to top job candidates, by encouraging your leaders to blog. When people outside the business read your company's thoughts on an area of expertise it helps to build the profile of the company. This is especially important for recruiting digital talent because savvy people want to work for innovative and creative companies.

So what makes good content?

- It appeals to its audience by being pitched at the right level.

- It grabs attention by solving a problem or shedding a new light on a topic.

- It goes out regularly, thereby fostering a sense of trust in its readers.

- It uses a mixture of media depending on how and where it will be consumed.

- It is interesting, with stories and examples.

Now I've got you thinking about content marketing you'll hopefully have some great ideas for how you can use it in your own HR department.

Create a rolling launch

When we in HR plan the launch of a new initiative, we tend to assume it has to be done in one massive push to make an impact. There are, however, two significant disadvantages to this:

- you have to wait until everything is ready, which slows you down (remember the agile product development process we looked at earlier), and

- there's so much noise going on elsewhere in the business, if you limit yourself to one promotional message delivered at one time you risk it being missed.

The alternative is to create a rolling launch.[82] In this way, you can also build new features and benefits into the change as you go along, which keeps the excitement going and gives you a steady stream of new things to talk about. An interesting question to ask yourself is: 'What's the minimum I could launch with? And how could I add more features as the months go by?' For instance, if you were launching a new performance review process you could start with the basics. Then you could add a 'career conversations' element to it, and later peer reviews, helping your HR team to provide interesting content about that. You're keeping the interest and attention alive.

One of your first steps for this is to get your early adopters lined up from the beginning. Hopefully you'll already have identified them through your permission marketing and the feedback you gained from your ongoing content distribution. In HR we don't think enough about early adopters, so how can you evangelise them and equip them with what they need to know? Perhaps you could give them access to early versions of your service and ask for feedback.

To help you, here's a handy summary of the main benefits of permission and content marketing in the

---

[82] https://www.fastcompany.com/3004920/10-steps-successfully-launching-new-product-or-service

context of a rolling launch, both for HR and your wider organisation.

Content and permission marketing benefits

Activity	Benefits to HR	Benefits to your organisation
Creation and distribution of expert content	Enhances your authority and creates trust	Broadens people's thinking and keeps them up to date
Creation of an early adopter database	You can communicate with those who are most interested	Avoids pestering those who don't care so much
Communication of ongoing improvements	Enables you to keep the interest alive, helps you to launch in bite-sized chunks, and promotes HR as the human experts (with human-scale communications)	More likely to end up with a service that works for them

You can see how moving away from a traditional, one-push marketing launch and towards a series of rolling mini-launches, accompanied by an ongoing content marketing programme, can be so effective. It's a more human, responsive, and respectful way to introduce users to an initiative, and in the end garners more positive attention from the right people. Good luck with yours.

Action point

- In your workbook, choose your next main initiative and list three ways you could make use of naming, permission and content marketing, and a rolling launch to promote it. You can download your workbook here: https://disruptivehr.com/thehrchangetoolkitworkbook.

Quick recap

- HR tends to focus on boring, admin-heavy, and one-off launches.

- A more effective approach is to replace them with these:

  o an initiative that has an appealing name for its target audience;

  o permission marketing that enables you to build a database of interested people;

  o content marketing that fosters trust in HR and helps your employees; and

  o a rolling launch that enables you to keep interest in your change alive.

Make Use of HR Technology

When you read earlier about why clunky, enterprise-wide HR systems are so terrible, you might have found yourself wondering what you should use instead. This chapter is the answer to that question. You'll find when you have the right technology working for you in a productive way, it will help you to change attitudes as well as working practices almost without you having to try.

I'll focus on apps because in my experience this is where HR can gain the most traction, but let's first consider why we in HR tend to be nervous about them. We worry about how we'll own the data they collect, that we'll confuse our employees by having too many of them, and that they only have limited functionality. This is understandable, because we're used to thinking of technology as something that should suit the needs of the business rather than those of the end user. However, one of my many criticisms of enterprise-wide systems is they rarely work well on our phones (if at all); and even if they have a mobile element they often simply take what we do on a desktop and replicate it on a phone. True mobile apps are the opposite, because when you take a 'mobile first' approach, the choice architecture you create will be suitable for how people work today. They also give you the opportunity to rethink the functionality as time goes by, as you get feedback from users.

There are more reasons why mobile apps are so brilliant compared to global systems. They're:

- relatively cheap;
- more impactful, which makes it easier to persuade people to use them;
- quick to implement;
- enhanceable as time goes by, which links in nicely with a rolling launch; and
- mobile and therefore flexible to develop and use.

What to look for in an app

There are many apps on the market that have been developed as mobile apps rather than as offline or desk-based systems. So how can you choose an app that will help you?

Make sure it does one thing well and go for a simple concept

I've seen some apps that cover objective setting, performance feedback, and reward all in one go, and that confuses people — I would avoid these. An alternative idea is to sign up for only one function of an app and add more features when everyone's become used to it. If you're worried about the app being too focused, bear in mind that in our personal lives we use an average of nine apps a day and 30 a month.[83] We're extremely comfortable with the concept of using one app for one task, and would rather be clear about how it helps us than to feel overwhelmed by too much detail.

Ask yourself if it's a pleasure to use

The best apps are highly intuitive and enable their users to get the best out of them within minutes: they're

---

[83] https://beta.techcrunch.com/2017/05/04/report-smart-phone-owners-are-using-9-apps-per-day-30-per-month/

polished, fast, and stable. A good way of checking if the app of your choice fulfils these criteria is to read its reviews and give it a test drive yourself. Would your managers and employees feel the same way about it as you do?

Ensure the in-app analytics are strong

It's important for you to be able to measure and analyse an app's use, so you're not at a disadvantage compared to using a traditional system. You want to know not only how many people have downloaded it, but also how they behave with it. Are they typically using one element and then coming out of it, in which case the flow doesn't work well? Or are they moving onto the next element each time?

Start by buying off-the-shelf apps

When you spend months developing your own app you're wasting time and energy especially at the beginning, because there are some brilliant ones already out there. You might feel a ready-made app doesn't meet all of your particular needs, but the vast majority of workplace apps are customisable in their look and feel. There are also obvious benefits to using tried-and-tested functionality rather than creating your own.

Some great apps for you to consider

What follows is a list of HR-relevant apps I've either used myself or know people who have, and that fulfil all the criteria above. Naturally it goes without saying that by the time you read this book more will have come onto the market and may be better than these ones, but it's useful for you to look at my recommendations because each one offers a different benefit to HR and will give you something to think about.

Attendify (for onboarding)

What I like about this app is that it was developed for events. If you've been to a conference which has its own app you'll be familiar with the functionality; it allows you to register, find out which speakers are on where, and connect with others. An HR Director friend of mine has put this to an interesting use — induction — and he loves it. He says it's incredibly easy to use, you can customise it with your own branding, and load rolling content to help your new starters to feel welcome and informed. This means that, as a new recruit, you can sign up and immediately connect to everybody in the organisation using your phone, asking all the newbie questions you need to while feeling in control. How about that as a contrast to the endless PowerPoints of the typical induction week? This app simply takes one aspect of induction, which is to help people feel connected to the company, and gives them a quick and easy way of doing it in their first few weeks. People may stop using it after then, but that's fine.

Looop (for learning)

Remember the days of the cumbersome 'learning management system'? You can kiss it goodbye with Looop, which is based on the idea that learning needs to happen when and where it suits the user. It's agile, extremely intuitive, and cost effective. Various HR clients of mine have adopted it, and what I love is that it encourages learning and development teams to focus less on training courses and more on curating learning content. This could be an online training programme, a webinar from the Chief Executive, short videos from key leaders, the best TED talks on a particular topic, interesting books and articles, interviews with external experts, and podcasts. You can use a range of media and group the content to make it easy to discover. It also looks professional and is easy to navigate.

Vibe (for engagement)

This is a new approach to employee engagement surveys, and without their inherent disadvantages. Vibe asks questions about how users feel about reward, learning, or communication in their organisations through pictures. The picture the employee chooses shows how they feel about the question. This image-based approach works well because it appeals to the emotional part of our brains rather than the analytical, logical one; this encourages a quicker and more intuitive response. HR teams who use this can gauge the mood of an organisation more effectively than traditional surveys enable them to do, and with real-time results being given direct to managers there's no more three-month wait for a complicated report to cascade down.

Smarp (for communications)

Going back to why HR finds it hard to create change, you'll remember we trust people 'like us' more than leaders. However, our fear in HR about letting employees loose on social media means we're missing a trick in not harnessing their collective influence as advocates of our businesses. Many of your employees will be proud of what their company is achieving, so Smarp makes it easy for them to disseminate content based on it to their friends and followers on their own social networks. It's also got great analytics so you can see what material is especially interesting to them.

Next Jump (for reward)

A completely different example of how HR can use apps is Next Jump. This is a rewards provider, and my favourite feature is its 'Top 10 Programme' because it recognises collaboration and generosity of spirit rather than individual achievements. It asks users one question: 'Who has helped you succeed?' There's a monthly leader board showing who's got the most enthusiasm for collaboration, which fosters helpfulness and co-operation, as well as showing an adult-to-adult approach to reward.

Clear Review (for performance management)

What I like about this app is that it incorporates the knowledge about what works and what doesn't in performance management. Instead of taking a broken annual process and putting it into a mobile app, they've created it from the ground up by building in elements such as frequent check-ins, real-time feedback, and peer reviews. It also contains videos on how to carry out these elements of performance management, which teaches people how to help their staff perform better.

Facebook Workplace (for communications and learning)

This is a mobile and web app that helps team members to stay connected, and for me it works because it's intuitive and familiar. It offers features such as Facebook Groups, Facebook Messenger, built-in audio and video calling, and access to Facebook's profiles, events, and live video tools. You can use it to offer learning, quizzes, and games, and it's already working with Starbucks, Royal Bank of Scotland, and Booking.com. A Workplace account is only visible to people in your team or company, is separate from their personal account, and there are always new features coming on board (Facebook is a brilliant role model for rolling launches).

Action point

- I could go on, but this is simply a varied selection of apps to show you what's possible and I encourage you to give some of them a go. In your workbook, list three of these apps (or any other you've heard is good) and test them out within your own HR team. You can download your workbook here: https://disruptivehr.com/thehrchangetoolkitworkbook.

Quick recap

- HR apps are a more effective way of using technology than clunky, enterprise-wide systems.

- Check first they meet your needs, but bear in mind they don't need to (and shouldn't) do everything.

- There are many great apps to choose from.

Measure the Impact

I'll be honest, I find the notion of measuring and assessing things a bit of a turn off — it's not really my style. But I know this is an area I need to pay attention to, and as a result I've made a conscious effort to learn about it because our approach to measurement is something we need to improve on in HR.

If you think about what data we've collected historically in HR it falls into three areas:

- *Core data* such as staff turnover rates, time to hire, sickness and absenteeism levels, and diversity statistics. While these are useful, for some HR teams their systems are so poor that even having accurate data at all seems unattainable. More importantly such data doesn't shed any light on *why* a certain situation exists.

- *Input measures* such as completion rates for performance reviews and attendance rates for training programmes. While these tell us something is happening they don't give us any sense of the impact, such as whether the training courses increase attendees' skills.

- *Commissioned research,* the most prominent of which is the annual engagement survey. This dinosaur is a colossal waste of HR's time and money and is hopefully on the way out. Any survey that only happens once a year, takes months to produce, and is limited to a snapshot of how employees feel at one moment in time has got to be pointless.

The element all three of these limited-use data sets has in common is central ownership by HR. We love that, don't we? Even though I can barely remember a single board meeting at which the HR data pack was discussed, we do enjoy having the information at our fingertips. The irony is that although we're the only ones who care about it, it doesn't even shape what we do in a meaningful way because it doesn't tell us what we need to know.

You can see why re-imagining how you measure the effects of change has got to be part of your movement away from cumbersome, controlled, and centralised HR processes and towards a more responsive and tailored approach. So how do you go about changing the way you measure things? Just as there's no one correct way to provide services to your internal customers, so there's no one set of measures that will tell you everything you want to know. What you need instead is a menu of measures and methodologies for collecting data which will result in a three-dimensional picture being built for you. Here's how to go about it.

Work with Marketing

The need for HR to work more closely with Marketing is one that crops up again and again, and measurement is no different. Marketing is the expert in understanding the impact of a strong, combined employer and consumer brand; it can therefore help you work out what measures to put in place to assess your employment brand in the marketplace, and how to gauge internal satisfaction levels from employees.

Check social media

It amazes me how many companies still don't check their ratings on Glassdoor, or even reply to comments on there. The platform tends to be seen as a slightly annoying commentary on our organisations that can at best be ignored and at worst dismissed as giving a distorted impression. When I'm approached by a potential HR client I always check their Glassdoor score in order to gain a sense of how they're doing. I find the lower the score, the less likely the client is to know it. And potential job candidates do check the platform. Are you seeing Glassdoor as a supplier of regular, useful data? And what about comments on other social media sites and the media?

Qualitative research

HR doesn't tend to undertake much qualitative research. If we do focus groups it's usually only at momentous points in our organisation's annual cycle, or if we're moving to a new office. We don't have a rolling programme, apart from possibly a regular 'meet the staff' session with the Chief Executive (one of the least helpful ways of finding out what people think). This is an area in which we need to smarten up. Why not hold regular research sessions with different groups of employees, at which they're asked their thoughts on how everything is for them? Whenever I've seen this happen people have welcomed it.

Pulse surveys

If you're going to do surveys at all, at least make them quicker and more regular than the traditional annual effort. Pulse surveys allow you to do that, and I'm glad to see they're becoming more common. They give you a rolling sample of people's views on particular topics, and also on how they're feeling. My favourite example is from Virgin Trains, a company that's done a huge amount of employee research and which said: 'We realised we were talking to 1,500 customers a day and our staff once a year.' Pulse surveys are a way of putting that right, and there are plenty of tools to use.

Make use of existing external data

People's LinkedIn profiles can give you an insight into how they're progressing (with their permission, of course). One company asked its staff to bring their profiles into their career conversations, as a way of prompting discussions around how they'd grown and developed over the year. This is a great example of HR not assuming it needs to own all the data, because the one thing that's likely to be up to date is an employee's LinkedIn profile (unlike our cumbersome learning management systems).

Proxy measures

If you cast your mind back to early in this book, you'll recall the four most significant challenges that organisations face today: they need their people to be more innovative, productive, collaborative, and agile. A helpful way of measuring movement in these areas is to identify proxy measures for them; these are indirect ways of seeing what's going on by using something that's been created for other purposes.

One example is consulting firm Nielsen, which created a mechanism by which its employees could register themselves as 'Ready to Rotate'. Originally developed to encourage people to gain wider experience throughout the company, it also gave Nielsen a window into how many people were open and willing to move. If this figure were to rise over time, it would tell them the organisation was becoming more agile. The main thing is to measure what matters to the business; if what's important is collaboration and agility, what proxy measures can you identify for these? Cisco, for instance, makes how many people someone emails, and is connected to, one of their criteria for promotion.

Action point

- You can see there's a wealth of data and resources for you to draw on, based on what's important for HR and your organisation to discover. In your workbook, list two behavioural movements you want to measure, and what ideas you have for doing so. You can download your workbook here: https://disruptivehr.com/thehrchangetoolkitworkbook.

Quick recap

- Traditionally, HR has been poor at gathering data which enables us to do things differently.

- There are a number of better alternatives for measurement:

  o working with marketing;

  o using social media;

  o qualitative research;

  o pulse surveys;

  o external data; and

  o proxy measures.

Know Your Limits

Although you've now got the information you need to plan and implement HR change, I imagine you might feel far from ready to dive in. In fact, I wouldn't blame you for experiencing a sense of overwhelm. I understand: I've lost count of the number of HR conferences I've attended at which I've lost the will to live as slide after slide flashes before my eyes — seven priority areas for change, six strategic focuses, nine issues to resolve — all with their cascading action plans. On top of that, for HR Managers in large organisations there's the ever-expanding number of Centres of Expertise to consider, each with its own reward, talent, performance, and recruitment plans. Add divisional plans and central programmes with their own data, analytics, and technology, and it's a recipe for overload.

This lack of focus in HR transformation worries me, because how can we possibly get across our message with impact if we take an 'all change welcome' approach? Remember Apple's product design process, in which it concentrates its efforts on a small number of beautifully designed pieces? Let's bring some of that into HR by choosing our battles. There's a simple process you can use to do this:

1. Identify the two or three changes you and your team will focus on relentlessly for the next three to six months. Choose them by considering:

    i.   the priorities of the business;
    ii. your end users and what they want, rather than the internal needs of HR; and
    iii. the changes that will most benefit HR's credibility.

2. Align your team behind the ones you pick, instead
    of filling a massive spreadsheet with strategic and
    operational priorities.

When people see that one thing and then another thing
is working — really working — they'll come to appreciate
that HR can achieve lasting and positive transformation.
You also need to think about how much change your
managers and employees can take at any one time, because it's probably less than you think. I hope this makes
the idea of shaking up HR and working practices in your
organisation feel easier for you.

Occasionally, though, there are certain situations in
which the best change you can make is to move yourself
elsewhere, as I'll explain below.

When to give up

This thought was prompted by a call I had from an HR
Manager who asked me to mentor her. She was the number two in her HR team at an investment bank, and although she had a remit to change HR so the company
could become more innovative and fast-paced, she was
hitting multiple barriers to doing so. The board wasn't
interested; the Chief Executive had no respect for HR
whatsoever and expected everything to be done his way;
her HR Director had minimal influence and was highly
risk averse; and her own team, which was primarily interested in preserving the status quo, was hostile towards
her. The 'problem' was that the company was doing well
financially and felt no imperative to change, despite her
argument that complacency was their number one risk.
Her situation couldn't be any worse, so I was puzzled as to
why she didn't seem to realise the futility of it.

After listening to her lament I asked her why she
didn't just leave. This drew a horrified response, so I

qualified it. 'Of course, I'm not saying you should definitely leave. It's your choice. But why not take your energies, talents, and insights to somewhere that sees the point of doing things differently?' And I meant it. So often I come across downtrodden HR professionals who have a sense of futility about them because they keep banging their head against a brick wall of resistance to change. I know how this feels. When I started at the BBC the advice I was given was to 'recalibrate' my expectations of how long it would take to change anything, from a year to two decades. That was no lie. By the end of my time there, what would have seemed like a failure in the beginning felt like a massive win. So I'm not an advocate of giving up at the first hurdle — far from it — but there are limits to what one human being can achieve without any support. If you haven't got a Chief Executive who's vaguely interested, an HR Director who's open to new ideas, leaders in the business who are curious, or any apparent business need to do anything differently, my advice is to go elsewhere. This may appear defeatist but look at what people in other departments do in these circumstances. When was the last time you saw an innovative Marketing or IT Manager hanging around after being told they're not allowed to try anything new?

We in HR sometimes lack the confidence to feel we're worth more than this, and while the notion of knowing when to give up might seem a negative one, I want it to be a wake-up call. If your situation is similar to the one above you deserve better, so if you can't get what you need where you are then I'd advise you to consider a different environment. Of course, initiating change in your company is always tough and not everyone's going to agree with you — you're going to have to do difficult things. But that's why you need at least some factors in your favour to give you a fighting chance of success.

Action point

- What two or three changes will you focus on at the beginning? Record them in your workbook. You can download your workbook here: https://disruptivehr.com/thehrchangetoolkitworkbook.

Quick recap

- Pick two or three changes to focus on at the beginning, instead of losing focus by overburdening yourself.

- Use the needs of the business, your end users, and HR's credibility to guide your priorities.

- There are times when it's best to look elsewhere, and the trick is to recognise when that is.

Section 7

A Test Case: Changing Performance Management

Now we've explored the various elements of changing HR, it's time for an example that pulls them all together. Let me introduce you to the MadeUp Engineering Company and its recently appointed HR Director, Sue Brightman. Having come from a progressive retailer, Sue's on a mission to transform the firm's HR practices from the parental model that's evolved over the years to a more adult-to-adult and responsive approach that will enable its employees to do their best work.

The company, a traditional family firm established in 1968, makes parts for car engines. It's still family-led but over the years has recruited professionals from its competitors and other manufacturing outfits. These new hires have been accompanied by a growing range of systems and processes, a situation which has led to the business losing some of its original entrepreneurial flair. Recently the company has moved into digital products, and this has fuelled both significant growth and a concern that it isn't well enough placed to recruit and retain new digital talent. Productivity isn't as good as it could be due to some recent quality issues, but thanks to these digital products the company is growing at around 10 percent each year and its prospects look good. It has 2,500 employees working across four sites in Europe; 55 percent are in engineering and operations, 20 percent in digital and R&D, 10 percent in sales and marketing, 10 percent in quality control, and 5 percent in finance and HR.

The business' HR approach is traditional: process-driven and compliance-oriented. Nothing exemplifies this more than its HR-led performance management system (PMS): objectives are set in April each year and cascaded down, and an annual review results in the allocation of employees into five grades. Bonuses for senior managers are up to 50 percent of their salaries and are paid according to the financial performance of their respective divisions. Other staff can earn between 10 and 20 percent of their salary on a combined basis of company and personal performance. There's no official guided distribution process but HR usually pushes back if one manager's grades appear to be too positive; this tends to cause some conflict during the HR-organised calibration sessions with managers.

Sue sees her top priorities as being the increase of productivity and making the company more attractive to digital talent. To do this she realises she needs to change the company's approach to performance management because of how outdated, cumbersome, and — most importantly — ineffective it is. Nor is she alone. In conversations with managers and employees, she's established that their feelings about the current system range from resignation to downright hostility ('waste of time', 'demotivating', 'too bureaucratic'). The problem is, her own HR team has historically worked hard to achieve a 98 percent completion rate and is nervous about tinkering with a system that, in their minds, works. The leadership team, however, has a more balanced response to her ideas: the CEO is keen on change as he sees little value in the current set-up, and is joined by the Marketing, Purchasing, and Digital Directors. The Sales Director and Operational Divisional Leaders are indifferent, with the Finance Director and second Operations Director being of the view that the company finally has a clear, solid system that everyone uses, so why change it?

Sue knows if she wants to change things she needs a plan. Here's what she decides she needs to do:

1. Prepare her own HR team and the organisation as a whole
2. Identify the main people she'll have to convince
3. Make her case for change via a pitch to leaders

4. Research her employees and create personas
5. Employ user-centred design techniques to deliver processes that people want
6. Decide what features to include in her new process
7. Pilot it to check it works
8. Launch it gradually with adequate support
9. Measure and tweak it as time goes by

It's quite a list, isn't it? Let's see how she goes about it and what we can learn from this.

Preparing the HR team and the organisation

Sue knows it's important not to drop any changes onto people without warning, so her first task is to prepare the ground throughout the company. Here's what she does.

- She sets up a workshop with her HR team of 30 to challenge them around the EACH principles (treating Employees as Adults, Consumers, and Human beings). In this she introduces them to what other companies are doing, shares data, and gets them to talk about their experiences. By doing this she's helping them to imagine how they might do things differently. Some of her team members turn out to be more enthusiastic than she'd assumed.

- For around three months before proposing anything new, she drip-feeds articles and insights into leaders' and managers' inboxes. These are focused on how ways of managing performance are changing, and how hard-to-find digital talent is looking for something different to what the business currently offers. She's priming people for change and educating her own HR team in the process.

- She carries out further research into current views of the company's performance management system and how it's operating throughout the business.

Who does Sue have to convince?

By discussing her plans on a one-to-one basis with key people, Sue identifies who she'll need to work extra hard to convince. These are her notes:

Finance Director

- Traditional view of HR — sees its value as driving compliance, managing transactions, and streamlining processes.

- Supported by a tight team that's worked for him for a long time and that doesn't tend to challenge him.

- Focused on controlling costs and will worry about anything that could escalate bonuses.

- Set in his ways, and not having experienced a better PMS elsewhere, is not interested in doing things differently.

Operations Director

- Negative view of HR apart from his HR Business Partner, whom he values for managing his transactions.

- Concerned about anything that takes up his time or affects the productivity of his team (on which he's measured). He's under pressure to raise profits on his side of the business because most of the growth is coming from digital.

- His managers are largely comprised of older men who are extremely loyal to him. Although they hate the current PMS because it's so time-consuming and doesn't add value, they're command-and-control in their style and would prefer not to bother with performance management at all if they could get away with it.

HR Business Partner for Operations

- Close relationship with the Operations Director and can influence him.

- Old-fashioned in style with a strong need for status. Sees herself as number two to Sue (applied for her role but didn't get it and is therefore a bit resentful; views anything Sue says with suspicion).

- Extremely busy and doesn't have time for anything new.

- Having built her reputation on achieving compliance and completing transactions for her managers, she's now worried about whether she can make the transition to a new role in which she's likely to be coaching managers instead.

These are the three main people Sue reckons will object to the changes she wants to make, and for different reasons. Some of their worries will be based on business issues such as escalating costs and time factors, and others will be personal, such as the fear of something new.

The pitch

Sue's first objective is to align the leadership team around the notion of a different way of managing performance. At this stage she realises it's not necessary to know what it will look like but that she must gain an agreement that *something* has to change, and she wants to gain permission from them to explore new options. She requests a 20-minute slot at the next board meeting in order to make her pitch, and when the time comes she tells a story. This story is not data-focused, but a spotlight focus on a typical manager who wastes many hours carrying out 12 Performance Management Reviews every year. He struggles to find time for them, he knows his people hate doing them, he can see the objective-setting process has become irrelevant, and he's far from convinced they improve his team's performance. It's a scenario everyone in the room recognises, especially the Operations Director who's aware this is how his managers experience it. She supports her opinions with powerful quotes from managers and employees, and backs them up with key nuggets of data from her research on costs, time, and rater bias: 78 percent of MadeUp's managers think the current system is a waste of time, over 75 percent have had the same rating for the last three years or more, and only nine percent believe that it's helped them to improve their performance. She presents a calculation that their PMS costs the business 600,000 euros a year, based on the time spent by managers and employees preparing for the performance meetings and the actual meetings themselves; the technology of the system; and HR's energy and focus.

This pitch has the effect of discrediting the current performance management system and we can see how she's addressed the concerns of her two key opponents: the Finance Director who wants to control costs, and the

Operations Director who wants to save time and deliver a less painful solution to his disillusioned managers. As part of it she appeals to the leaders' herd mentality, by outlining how many companies, including one of Made-Up's main customers and also its competitors, are experimenting with new ways of managing performance more effectively. Surely they wouldn't want to be left behind? She also makes use of this mentality with her HR Business Partner for Operations. She knows it will be difficult to persuade her to come on board, so she decides to leave her out of the change by not trying to convince her at this stage. She trusts she'll be won over eventually.

Finally she gives a call to arms, which is that the company needs to sustain its growth and therefore must urgently find a way of managing performance that's less time-consuming, more cost effective, and that helps people to work more effectively. In her view this is down to managers and staff having better quality conversations, and it will also help the business appeal to digital talent. As a result she receives the go-ahead to come back with worked-up proposals of how a new system could operate.

The design

Sue's next task is to get inside her employees' heads so she can understand what matters to them. From examining broad demographic data and working with her HR colleagues, she identifies four typical employee personas; as you'll remember, these are fictional but based on a knowledge of the company's workforce. She plans to use them as inspiration for change and also to test out prototypes.

Mark — manager of a large operational team

- Age 51.
- Been with MadeUp for 17 years.
- Likes football and fishing.
- Reads newspapers and watches TV.
- Uses his smartphone mainly for calls (doesn't like email).
- *Wants:* job security, protected benefits, and regular recognition for his hard work. Isn't interested in promotion or any of the management development programmes he's been sent on.
- *Fears:* being out of his comfort zone and anything that might make him look stupid. Nervous about how digital is challenging the traditional focus of operations.
- *Cares about:* the company (he's proud of what it's achieved), his team, and their work.

Sue's angle with Mark will be to show him how a new way of managing performance can be used to recognise when someone does a good job more regularly than once a year, thereby tapping into his desire to be appreciated for his experience and expertise.

Jean — digital product developer

- Age 35.
- Been with MadeUp for two years.
- Married with one small child.
- Loves live music and keeping fit, when she's got time.

- Watches and reads everything via apps on her tablet and phone.

- *Wants:* interesting projects, salary increases, and to become a manager in the next 12 months (will probably leave if she doesn't as she gets plenty of offers).

- *Fears:* boring work that doesn't challenge her or keep her skills up to date.

- *Cares about:* earning more so she can pay the mortgage and childcare bills, and being stimulated by new and interesting work.

Sue's angle with Jean will be to convince her that more up-to-date ways of managing performance can make her work more interesting and challenging, and will also allow her the opportunity to pitch regularly for promotions and rewards.

Sam — front-line supervisor

- Age 45.
- Been with MadeUp for 10 years.
- Married with two school-aged children.
- Loves socialising with friends and participating in clubs — a people person.
- Spends time on social media via his phone while he rushes from one event to the next.
- *Wants:* lots of contact with his team and customers.
- *Fears:* being sat at a desk on his own and hates paperwork.
- *Cares about:* making people feel good.

Sue's angle with Sam will be to help him realise quick-fire and immediate performance review sessions will give him the contact he loves with his staff, without taking up more of his scarce time.

Jules — the marketing executive

- Age 25.
- Been with MadeUp for two years, having joined as a post-graduate.
- A millennial.
- Loves social media and going to clubs with friends, also supports a couple of charities close to her heart.
- *Wants:* to be promoted rapidly, to influence the direction of the company, and to have regular feedback on her performance.
- *Fears:* being ignored or overlooked (she'll leave if so).
- *Cares about:* what her peers think and producing quality work that's valued.

Sue's angle with Jules will be to emphasise the excitement of moving to a new process that will give her regular opportunities for feedback (including from her peers) and promotion, and to contribute to the company's direction.

You can see how Sue's created her personas with her company in mind. She recognises the business isn't large enough to warrant segmenting her employees for the new PMS, but that she still needs to take a different communication tack with each group.

Making use of user-centred design

Sue also wants to take a user-centred design approach to creating change, and to do this she realises she needs to know more about how both operational and front-line staff work. She pays a visit to observe Mark running a team meeting, because it interests her to learn how regular team conversations might work as an alternative to annual one-to-one reviews. She also spends a day with Sam, seeing how he works with his manager and team. Finally she gets a group of digital developers together to ascertain their views on how they'd like to be recognised and rewarded.

In addition she holds an open hackathon by inviting staff, leaders, and marketing and product design people. In it she asks them a question: 'How can HR help you to perform better?' Through this, she gains their ideas on what matters to them and what they would change if they had the chance. When it's over she concludes that instead of their current PMS, an approach with the following three key features would work much better.

Feature One: a new approach to objective-setting

Sue knows most people aren't as excited by business metrics as leaders are and that annual, cascaded-down SMART objectives are irrelevant in a fast-moving business environment. There will therefore be a move to communicating business ambitions and results on a quarterly basis, which will give everyone a richer sense of what problems the company faces and where it's heading. Minimal metrics will be involved, with more attention given to stories focusing on the company's vision, values, customers, and employees. The CEO will communicate this to managers by email and will also visit a different site quarterly in order to share objectives with staff. Local managers will then communicate these insights with their own teams, making sure the data is relevant for their particular area of the business.

Feature Two: improving performance

The new performance management process will be a simple one, with two aspects to it. The first is a move to frequent check-ins between employees and line managers; these will be short, undocumented conversations that will encourage a responsive and agile approach to performance improvement. She knows she will need to test these and isn't yet sure how often they should take place or how to structure them, but is clear they'll provide timely feedback, be quick, and not too onerous. The second is to introduce team performance conversations, or peer-to-peer reviews, as part of a team's normal meeting cycle. These will enable employees to reflect on their own performance as part of a team discussion, instead of limiting the feedback to one-to-one. She knows from her research that millennials like this approach and that teams that hold regular reviews, in which they critique their performance in an open and honest way, outperform those that don't. This new process will clearly require a change of heart by most people.

Feature Three: helping people to develop their careers

The final feature of her plan is to help people to develop their careers by having career conversations with their managers. She's not yet sure how often they should be, but she knows they'll be worthwhile. She'll also ask leadership teams to include a 'Talking Talent' session within their regular team meetings, rather leaving this to an annual talent review. This way they'll be constantly aware of who's ready for a move or to widen their experience, any upcoming projects that may be suitable for them, and challenges other leaders are facing within their own teams.

The pilot

Sue decides to carry out four pilots to test her new features:

- team performance conversations within one of the operational teams;
- frequent check-ins within one of the digital teams;
- career conversations within the marketing team;
- 'Talking Talent' sessions within the leadership team.

She wants to get these kicked off pretty much immediately and has chosen a three-month time horizon in which to carry them out. Having set up a regular feedback loop between the treatment groups and her own team, and a regular Monday morning session within HR to monitor progress like Apple does, she's confident any tweaks or extra support that are needed will become apparent and that learnings will come to the surface quickly.

What does she discover? That the concepts are good — people like frequent check-ins and career conversations. However, managers are struggling to carry them out and need more support. Team performance conversations are popular in theory, but employees are finding it hard to know how to facilitate them because of their traditional command-and-control approach, especially for managers who aren't used to critiquing their own performance. It also turns out both managers and staff are worried about how their bonuses will be calculated if there's no grade to go by. So while the pilot is running, Sue puts in place some support for managers. She creates a series of short videos showing them how to carry out a frequent check-in, and what a career conversation could look like. In order to improve confidence with facilitating peer reviews in team performance conversations, she institutes some more formal training because it's a focused skill.

Sue would love to re-evaluate the company's bonus scheme as well, because she knows it's not motivating and rewarding enough, but based on what people in the pilot groups are telling her about their bonus worries she sees she doesn't have enough support for change in this area. She decides giving line managers the discretion to award pay rises and bonuses is just too scary and risky for the business initially, so she introduces the idea of a reward calibration session at the end of the year. In this, instead of the traditional battle by managers over grades for their teams, the focus will be on what the right level of pay is for each individual according to their skills, and how meaningful a cash bonus is for them. Could other rewards be more useful, such as opportunities to work on projects, a promotion, or greater flexibility with time off? The purpose of this is to have a richer conversation about pay and reward, and to reassure staff that their managers aren't making these decisions in isolation.

The launch

Now Sue's carried out the pilots that show her concepts are good ones and put in place support for managers, it's time for her to launch her new performance management process. Prior to this, though, she tests out some naming ideas with the pilot treatment groups. They land on the name 'Better Conversations', because it does what it says on the tin and underlines the concept of a two-way discussion as opposed to an assessment.

She then arranges for the CEO to address the whole company at a launch event, at which he shares the pivotal conversations in his career that have helped him to perform better. This story-based approach lends a personal edge to his presentation. He also emphasises how important it is for his people to have conversations that will help the business to grow, and to encourage them all to perform at their best. As a climax towards the end he announces there will be no more grades — this is the new default position and is a clear, dramatic statement.

After this event Sue decides to introduce Better Conversations through a nine-month rolling launch, because she knows it would be too confusing to introduce all four new conversation types at once. Through this she's shrinking the change and making it feel manageable, instead of onerous and difficult. She doesn't want to risk her transformation failing at this stage by expecting too much of people too soon.

She starts with frequent check-ins

Sue kicks things off by focusing on frequent check-ins, describing it as a five-minute conversation a manager could have once a week with each of their staff members to recognise something they've done well. The reason she starts with this is a clever one: most managers enjoy giving praise and will find it easier to move to this habit than if they were asked to do something that makes them feel uncomfortable. It's a positive and easy place to begin, with a feel-good reward built in. Also, by shrinking the task to one type of activity for five minutes, she's made it manageable — we can all find time to do that in our week. It's important to note that, at this stage, Sue doesn't demand everyone take part but simply asks people to give it a go. She's keen this should be a voluntary process, because otherwise HR will fall back into its traditional role as the policeman rather than the enabler. Those managers who express an interest are sent random emails from HR with prompts reminding them to have a five-minute conversation, and are primed through the inclusion of sample questions to get them started.

To incentivise managers to carry out these five-minute feedback sessions, she puts up posters around the company. These contain fun facts about what can be achieved in five minutes, and quotes about great conversations in history; this is her way of using content marketing in a way that all employees will read and appreciate. Through this she builds an energy around the launch and employees start to talk about it. She also taps into everyone's herd mentality by recording a video of the pilot treatment group discussing how easy and fun they found the frequent check-ins, and how beneficial they were.

Sue builds the change gradually, all the while checking in with teams who are using this process, gathering feedback and evidence of success. After a period of time she carries out a sampling exercise: this tells her 80 percent of employees have had at least one conversation with their manager that week. She announces this through the company e-newsletter and gives praise to those who are participating, with the aim of encouraging those who aren't. When the latter sees how 'everyone else' is doing it, how easy it is, and how it's helping to improve performance, it stimulates their curiosity about taking part. Alongside this the CEO talks about the conversations he's had with his leaders, which builds momentum.

She then introduces team performance conversations

Three months have passed and there's an energy around the launch; more people are starting to take part and HR is receiving great feedback. Sue's team is feeling good about making change fun to engage with instead of frightening, and she therefore decides to introduce team performance conversations next. She starts by encouraging members of the leadership team to adopt these sessions so as to encourage others. In them they set objectives for the month, check in with how they're doing, and critique themselves. In order to facilitate this she helps the Chief Executive to hold a team peer-to-peer review. She also emails managers to explain what they are, to give positive feedback from the pilot, and to add that the Chief Exec and his team are doing them already. As part of this communication process, she also makes use of permission marketing in which she asks managers to let her know when they're ready to take part, because she wants them to feel a desire to be part of the gang rather than pressured into it.

In the background she provides training on how to facilitate a team review and has trained her HR team in this as well, so they can offer help. She sends round articles and TED talks on how to make a success of peer-to-peer reviews, and has filmed a live internal review, sharing highlights from it together with the team members discussing its pros and cons. Then, when she's got a critical mass of people doing them, she starts to drip-feed additional statistics into her communications, such as the fact that the best performing teams in the company are carrying out these reviews; the underlying message is, 'What are you missing out on by not taking part?'

Finally, she introduces career conversations

After another three months have passed, Sue turns her attention to career conversations. Again, prior to launching them she carries out some content marketing aimed at employees who want to build their careers. She includes material about how to grow and develop, as well as videos of people in the pilot treatment group talking about why career conversations matter and what they did for them. She then has the CEO announce a new default position: growth isn't optional. While doing so, he tells personal stories about how he and his leadership team have continued to learn new things even though they're at the tops of their professions.

Sue also provides useful information about the three types of career conversation it's possible to have: how to go deeper, how to go wider, and how to go up. The first caters for employees who are long-serving experts by focusing on the benefits of deepening their knowledge and skills, the second for those who want to learn more but aren't necessarily interested in promotion, and the third for those who want to be promoted. This supports the company's belief that continuing to be curious and to grow is vital for a business in the digital age. It also addresses the diverse needs of her employee personas. Alongside this she asks, 'What kind of conversation do you want?' This allows her to gather insights about what proportion of employees are interested in what kind of growth.

She tells managers she wants these career conversations to be held ideally every three months, but that six months will do at a push. She leaves employees and managers to agree this between them, so the desires of career-focused millennials are catered for alongside those who are less ambitious. Managers can either pick a single time frame for all their team members or adjust it to suit individual needs. She also provides support for managers, with conversation prompts and videos showing what good looks like.

Continuous measurement and tweaking

Sue knows that in a user-centred design context, a service or process is never 'finished'. So she sets up a chat room for people to share the conversations they've had, and regular focus groups to check how Better Conversations is working. All new starters now receive a welcome pack explaining the company's approach, telling them they need to ask their manager for a career conversation at the time that seems right for them. This begins to shift the onus from manager to employee, which is appropriate in a business recruiting increasing amounts of digital talent. In fact it goes so well over time the digital team announces it wants to trial a feedback app called Clear Review, which seems to work well.

Now Better Conversations is up and running successfully, Sue's task is to keep measuring the results and to continue to tweak it. The MadeUp Engineering Company has moved from a performance management process that was controlling, retrospective, and burdensome, to one that's responsive, results-oriented, and easy to carry out.

Section 8

20 Changes You Can Make Right Now

In the spirit of making change easy and less intimidating, I've created a list of 20 changes you can make immediately. You'll not want to do them all right away but why not pick a handful that appeal and give them a go?

1. Change your employee handbook from a legal document to a marketing one which focuses on who you are, what your approach is, and how you treat people like adults. This is a quick win and will have a significant impact on new starters in your organisation. We put together a guide for a client that went down well because it references information employees need to know, but doesn't go into a lot of detail. For instance, the expenses policy summary is: 'Act in our best interests and spend our money like it's your own'.

2. Embrace Glassdoor. Look at it regularly, take it seriously, and discuss it with your team. Respond to people who post on there, encourage all employees to post on it themselves, and expect leaders and managers to see it as a vital element of your consumer and employer marketing.

3. Change your annual engagement survey to a pulse-style approach. Send it monthly to a sample of your employees and ask fewer questions.

4. With your HR team, create your employee personas. Then use them to help you design your HR products and influence how you communicate with your employees.

5. Get rid of annual performance ratings. Stop hanging onto them and just do it.

6. Stop talking about HR services and start seeing them as products instead.

7. Structure your HR team around the three or four key experiences you want to create, rather than the services and policies you want to produce.
8. Pilot and introduce some HR apps.
9. Try a new learning approach. Instead of pushing out training programmes, provide and curate learning content, maybe using an app like Looop.
10. Host some regular 'talking talent' sessions with clusters of managers as an alternative to the annual talent review. Just get them going.
11. Make friends with some digital people in your company and start to understand concepts like user-centred design (UXD), minimum viable products, and agile product design.
12. Choose three new or improved HR products/services to focus on for the next six months.
13. Hold an HR jargon amnesty by asking your employees and team what names and terms annoy them the most. Then stop using them.
14. Start a small content marketing programme by sharing the best of the latest articles and TED talks about people leadership.
15. Change your diversity targets to those that express the maximum percentage of homogeneity you're after, rather than a minimum percentage of different groups.
16. Hold an HR hackathon to discover the rules preventing your people from providing the best service to their clients.
17. Identify five micro influencers in your organisation and supply them with data and insights for a three-month period.

18. Carry out a quick 'credibility check' within your HR team.
19. Check your five most extensively used HR processes against your external brand promise. Do they support or undermine it?
20. Read the requirements from your regulator in detail and check how much scope you have to change your processes as a result.

Section 9

Essential Reading

Throughout this book I've referred to many others that have shaped my thinking around HR change; I really couldn't have written it without them. I'm sure you're a busy person so I've not included all of them here, but I can guarantee it will be worth your while to read the following (there's also an app called Blinkist which summarises the latest business books for further recommendations).

Thinking Fast and Slow by Daniel Kahneman

This is Kahneman's theory of our two system brains, System One (automatic, intuitive, and effortless) and System Two (reasoning, deliberate, and focused). So much of what we do in HR requires our leaders and employees to use System Two, and yet we neglect to recognise that most of the time they can't help reacting through System One. If you've ever wondered why traditional HR performance management, reward, or change management processes fail to produce the results you desire, this book gives you the science behind the reasons. It doesn't provide a blueprint for changing your approach but it will help you build the case for making that change.

The Power of Habit by Charles Duhigg

This is another book about how to change behaviour that's worth a read. Too often we try to achieve behavioural change through imposing HR processes or systems, ignoring how the behaviours (or habits) have become established in the first place. If we understand this — and Duhigg explains a three-step loop of 'cue, routine, and reward' — then it can help us change behaviour. The most interesting bit for HR professionals is Part Two of the book, in which Duhigg focuses on the habits of organisations and how to create lasting change at an enterprise-wide level. If you're looking for fresh insights into delivering organisational change without having to create yet another HR process, you'll enjoy this.

Nudge by Richard Thaler

The definitive work on what shapes human behaviour and how we can use small behavioural 'nudges' to influence our leaders and employees. It's not an easy read, and there are points at which you have to work hard to apply his approaches to a business setting, but it's worth it in order to get your head around different approaches to leading change.

Mindset by Carol Dweck

Dweck's central theory is that the beliefs we have about ourselves permeate every part of our lives. She crystallises this into two dominant types of beliefs: a fixed mindset and a growth mindset. A fixed mindset comes from the assumption that our qualities are carved in stone — who we are is who we are, period. Characteristics such as intelligence, personality, and creativity are fixed traits and not capable of being developed. A growth mindset comes from the belief that our basic qualities can be cultivated through effort. Although people differ greatly in aptitudes, talents, interests, or temperaments, everyone can change and grow through application and experience. The importance of this book for HR professionals is it recognises what holds people back from learning new things, how we respond to criticism and praise, and why some people feel more able to change than others. This is useful in helping us determine the types of people we recruit or promote, and how we can begin to help our employees to build a growth mindset to enable change.

Drive by Dan Pink

It amazes me that despite this classic having been around for nearly 10 years, our reward and recognition practices still rely predominantly on dangling financial carrots. This book provides us with more proof than we can handle that monetary incentives rarely, if ever, improve long-term performance, and that even worse, they can diminish performance, crush creativity, and encourage unethical behaviour. Sadly, Pink's convincing alternatives for motivating performance (mastery, purpose, and autonomy) are still largely absent from our performance and reward mechanisms.

Switch by Chip and Dan Heath

I love this book. It starts with a helpful image of how managing change is like a rider sitting atop an enormous elephant. Just as this rider doesn't have the strength to force the elephant to do what he wants, so we don't have the strength to overcome our intrinsic and emotional responses. We need to develop tactics to move the elephant that aren't apparent in typical change programmes. This book lays them out, with great stories to bring them to life.

What Matters Now by Gary Hamel

The book is described as a multi-faceted agenda for building organisations that can win in a world of relentless change, ferocious competition, and unstoppable innovation. Hamel asks, 'What are the fundamental, make-or-break issues that will determine whether your organisation thrives or dives in the years ahead?' He suggests five: values, innovation, adaptability, passion, and ideology. It's enjoyable to read as Hamel writes with an orator's passion and richness of language, but what most resonated with me was his views on building innovation from the ground up. Essential reading for HR Directors who are tempted to embark on a top-down programme of change.

Wilful Blindness by Margaret Heffernan

In this book, Heffernan argues that the biggest threats and dangers we face are the ones we don't see — not because they're secret or invisible but because we're deliberately blind to them. She examines this phenomenon and traces its imprint on our private and working lives, and within governments and organisations, and then goes on to outline some of the mechanisms, structures, and strategies that institutions and individuals can use to combat it. The book is brilliantly written and super smart, and you'll be particularly interested in Chapter 10 which explains why bonuses are so damaging.

Yes! by Robert B. Cialdini

As an HR Director my role often involved persuading people to do things they might not want to do. This book was an eye-opener for me as to why we make the choices we do, and how small, less obvious behavioural nudges can be amazingly effective in achieving change. While the focus is more on consumer than employee behaviour, the lessons are infinitely transferable. It's full of practical tips, based on academic research, and shows how the psychology of persuasion can provide valuable insights for anyone in HR.

About the Author

Lucy Adams is on a mission to help organisations bring their human resources departments into the 21st century. Through her agency, Disruptive HR, she aims to provoke the HR community into creating new ways to support businesses in today's complex and ambiguous world. In doing so she challenges leaders and HR professionals to learn from sources as varied as management theory, consumer organisations, marketing, digital product development, neuroscience, and the latest thinking on motivation and reward.

Lucy describes herself as a 'recovering HR Director', having been in front-line roles and on the boards of some major organisations including the BBC.

Along with her business partner, Lucy runs workshops and consults on many topics within the HR arena. She specialises in helping HR and other business professionals to step back from their old assumptions about motivating people, and to find more creative and effective ways of engaging employees.

As part of this she's started a movement to shake up HR around the world. Central to it is her newly launched The Disruptive HR Club, a special online network for HR people who are tired of traditional approaches and want something different. It's a fun and friendly platform in which to learn, grow, gain practical support, and engage not only with Disruptive HR but also with other like-minded people from organisations around the globe. Find out more at www.disruptivehr.com.

As well as being a consultant Lucy is an acclaimed speaker on various topics related to HR and leadership.

Here are some comments from those she's entertained and informed:

'You managed to do that difficult thing of getting people to think more broadly about their profession, sharing fresh thinking from other companies, and weaving this into a stimulating and entertaining narrative – great result!' *Accenture*

'You were fantastic! The levels of enthusiasm, engagement and participation from the audience were unprecedented with this group. I found you insightful, educational, inspirational...' *Deloitte*

'THANK YOU for a great session yesterday — you absolutely nailed it.' *Standard Life*

'You were great! Exactly what we needed. The feedback about you was glowing.' *IBM*

If you're interested in having Lucy help your organisation turn HR thinking on its head, or if you'd like to ask her about speaking at your next event, visit her website www.disruptivehr.com.

Lucy Adams

www.disruptivehr.com

Also by Lucy Adams
HR Disrupted

HR has lost its way and needs to find a new direction. The central question this book sets out to answer is: *If we are to survive and thrive in this new, volatile business world, how do we lead, manage, engage and support our employees in a radically different way?*

HR departments, and companies, need to transform their approach. This entails not simply tinkering with the process or the mechanics, but taking a completely fresh look at the entire scenario.

To achieve this change, Disruptive HR has three pillars:

1. Treating employees as adults not children
2. Treating employees as consumers or customers (not a one-size-fits-all approach)
3. Treating employees as human beings

EACH: **E**mployees as **A**dults, **C**onsumers and **H**uman beings. (Each of us is different, each of us deserves better.)

So what happens when you read this book? First, there's the lightbulb moment: 'I do that and I hadn't even realised it'. Then you'll see what this means for you and your organisation, with practical tools, ideas and techniques so you can start making changes immediately.

And finally, the hard bit: this book will help you introduce this new thinking to others in your business.

Lucy Adams is on a mission to help organisations bring their human resources departments into the 21st century. Through her agency, Disruptive HR, she aims to provoke the HR community into creating new ways to support businesses in today's complex and ambiguous world. Lucy was HR Director at the BBC during one of its most turbulent periods. In her five-year tenure Lucy witnessed four Director Generals come and go, oversaw the move to the Salford site, and coped with numerous and very public crises, including executive payoffs and the Savile scandal.

Practical Inspiration Publishing 2017, £14.99

ISBN 9781910056509